Freedom *in* His Story

How Jesus Can Use Your Past to Bring His Peace

ELLEN SCHUKNECHT

with

DEBI JOLMA

RIVERSTONE GROUP
PUBLISHING

Freedom in God's Story is a relevant and timely word of truth for all believers! As followers of Jesus we have a mandate to not merely be saved, but to thrive with the abundant life Jesus promises. As we abide in Christ, His life wells up in us and overflows to others, becoming the source of renewal and revival for the next generation. Ellen Schuknecht uses personal stories and testimonies to show how others have made this journey, how they have moved from anxiety to joy, from wilderness to freedom, from struggles and darkness to light and love.

> **— Dr. Mike Chrasta**
> Author, Co-director of a Prayer Ministry &
> Strategic Marketplace Intercessor

Ellen has a naturally genuine way of getting to the heart of what truly matters, impacting those she encounters and our culture today. This exceptional quality is something I noticed about her when we first met. Since then, her grace and wisdom have blessed me. In *Freedom in God's Story*, Ellen Schuknecht shares heartfelt personal accounts that showcase the extraordinary ways God uses adversity to strengthen our faith and shape our character. Ultimately, this book is a powerful reminder that even in our darkest moments, the promise of an abundant life in Jesus prevails. Having experienced a radical transformation in my own life through Jesus, I know firsthand the joy and freedom of living in God's story. Whether you're in the lowest valley or on the highest mountain, you'll find hope and peace within the pages of this book. Thank you, Ellen, for reminding us that true freedom is available right now!

> **— Jeff Jerina**
> Author of *Faith Without Fear*
> Founder & Host of *Men Unplugged*

DEDICATION

To all of our grandchildren - the next generation. You are each his workmanship, created in Christ Jesus for good works, which God prepared beforehand, that you should walk in them. (Ephesians 2:10) Let your light for Christ shine brightly. It can change the world.

ELLEN'S GRANDCHILDREN:

Josiah – Your name means *"Yahweh supports."* God has created you strong and steady, someone others can trust and rely on. With God as your support, you will thrive in all of your endeavors.

Kate – Your name comes from the Greek word *"katharos"* meaning pure. Purity of heart is the light by which you will thrive and bring hope to many.

Jude – Your name means *"praised."* You will thrive as a light that points others away from darkness into God's light where their hope is renewed.

Hadassah – Your name means *"myrtle tree"* which symbolizes peace, love, and prosperity. He created you with a tenacious drive and you will thrive in the love of God.

Greta – Pearl. Your name is a derivative of Gertrude, meaning *"spear of strength,"* as is your great grandmother, Kerttu. Like her, you have a strength of will, or sisu, by which you will thrive.

William – Your name has German roots. Will signifies resolute. Helm refers to a helmet. You are a *resolute protector*, and you will thrive as a leader others trust to follow.

Isaac – Your name in Hebrew means *"he will laugh, he will rejoice."* God has blessed you with a beautiful smile and heartfelt laughter. You will thrive in a joy that draws many to Jesus.

Asa – Your name in Hebrew means *"healer."* You came into the world struggling to live, but God healed you and you will thrive as you bring healing of heart to many.

Elsie – Your name means noble - *"pledged to God."* Your gentle, thoughtful nature sets you up to thrive in loving relationships and God's good purpose for you.

Alma – In Hebrew your name means *"nourisher and kind."* In Spanish it means "soul." You will thrive as a compassionate person who brings soul nourishment to many.

Bethlehem – Your name means *"house of bread."* God created you to thrive as a source of strength for others by encouraging them with your enthusiasm and joyful nature.

DEBI'S GRANDCHILDREN:

Tyler – Your name means *"tiler – or maker of roofs"* A house builder. God has created you to oversee and protect. You will thrive as a leader and an encouragement to all those around you.

Grace – Your name in Latin means *"goodness and generosity."* God has given you a tender heart. You will thrive as a generous, forgiving, and loyal child of God.

CONTENTS

Introduction 7

Chapter 1: *Jesus Take the Pen* 13

Chapter 2: *Writing Resilience* 21

Chapter 3: *Writing Faith* 27

Chapter 4: *Writing Truth* 35

Chapter 5: *Writing Healing* 43

Chapter 6: *Writing an Escape* 51

Chapter 7: *Writing Vision* 61

Chapter 8: *Rewriting History* 73

Chapter 9: *Writing Peace that Surpasses Understanding* 81

Chapter 10: *Writing Strength* 91

Chapter 11: *Writing Fortitude* 99

Chapter 12: *Writing Love* 109

Chapter 13: *Writing Forgiveness* 121

Chapter 14: *Writing Hope* 131

INTRODUCTION

*"The night is far gone; the day is at hand. So then let us cast
off the works of darkness and put on the armor of light".*
Romans 13:12

*"The wilderness has a way of curing our illusions about
ourselves and teaching us to depend more and more on God."*
Marlena Graves, A Beautiful Disaster

My story started in 1952.

That means that I grew up right as the US was coming out of the most tragic war it had ever fought, and I became an adult in the late 60's and early 70's, right when the nation was facing nation-wide discord, of anger and violence, of war, and a societal dismantling of prevailing values.

I've seen a lot.

The early chapters of my story were written as I watched friends search for peace and love through drugs, music, and sexual freedom. I struggled to understand how so many traded in their values, their hopes, and their freedom in exchange for a few fun hours or days. I watched many, including my older sister, fall into deep disillusionment because no matter how hard they tried, true peace and freedom seemed to evade them.

Yet, it was in the midst of this void, that God wrote a better story.

Just when things seemed futile, when culture seemed lost, and when the future of teenagers and young adults seemed hopeless, Pastor Chuck Smith's ministry exploded in what is now called the ***Jesus Revolution***.

Through this spiritual revival, millions of people's stories were rewritten by a God of freedom, of peace, and of hope.

This same God is still writing better stories today.

Today, our culture is more fractured than ever. The stories people tell are of anxiety, of hopelessness, of despair. But they long for bigger stories, better stories full of freedom and peace, with lasting meaning and purpose.

But how can these stories be rewritten when so many seem to be stumbling around in a so-called wilderness, full of discord and unrest? And how can we all find freedom, peace, and hope like so many have before?

It's not new for God to rewrite stories.

Time and time again, he finds people right when their story is at its messiest, right when they are lost in the wilderness with seemingly no hope of redemption, and that's when he gets to work.

That's when he starts to write.

> "Behold, I am doing a new thing; now it springs forth, do you not perceive it? I will make a way in the wilderness and rivers in the desert. The wild beasts will honor me, the jackals, and the ostriches, for I give water in the wilderness and rivers in the desserts, to give drink to my chosen people, the people whom I formed for myself that they might declare my praise." (Isaiah 43:19-21)

God's stories are the exact opposite of the stories we see in the world. His stories don't let circumstances shake us, but instead, they form and revive us. He breaks down our facades and strips us of our self-sufficiency. He teaches us how to depend on Him. Stories that seem to be full of decline and loss are often the very stories where seeds of revival will break open and grow.

God's stories allow us to live in hope. They are full of unexplainable peace, even when they are written in a shaking, confusing, anxious world. Mark Sayers explains it beautifully in his book, a *non-anxious presence*.

> *"Without God, wildernesses, both literal and figurative, are terrible places. With God, they become tools in our Savior's hands. Schools of spiritual growth. The wilderness reveals the direction of our hearts. Our character is indeed shown in moments of challenge."* (pg. 116-117)

God forms people after his own heart in the wilderness, writing their stories as people who desire to be shaped by him and set apart for his purposes.

Stories are incredibly impacting, and we each have one.

Your story matters because God is writing it.

And His story can set you free.

> *"So if the Son has set you free, you will be free indeed."*
> John 8: 36

DEBI

When Ellen first approached me about the idea of her writing a book about our personal stories and how God brought us hope and freedom through them (not in spite of them), I said no way. No way was I going to put my story out there, with all of its pain and struggle, with all of the mistakes I have made.

For many months, I resisted. But God kept nudging my soul.

What if my story could help someone to find hope in a difficult time?

What if my own kids and grandkids could be inspired by the story God has written for my life?

What if writing this was what God wanted?

What if?

I started discussing with Ellen the idea of writing my story. Of putting words on paper. And she suggested we start by just talking and pondering, discussing what we both felt led to say about each of our stories. So I took that one tiny step.

Ellen has gotten into the habit of getting up really early– like 5 am early– to spend time in the quiet, thinking and praying. She has learned that at that time of day when her heart and mind are free of noise and distractions, the Lord speaks to her. She often writes down what she hears, and those "morning ponderings" have become the basis for many of the discussions we have had about this book.

And so, day by day, pondering by pondering, this book developed in our minds. The coming pages are full of those ponderings, of the many conversations we've had on walks and over meals, and both of our reflections on them.

We have worked on *Freedom in His Story* over many, many months. Years even. This book is full of the things we have both thought of and talked about together as God has continued to set us free, despite our age, despite all the reasons we could grow anxious and discouraged. As we spent time looking back on our own lives, and listened to the stories of others, we have seen common themes of how God strengthens and refines his people through difficulty and struggle.

Even now, I feel vulnerable putting this book out there. I am worried about what people will think, what people will say.

But I am also convinced that God wrote my story for a purpose– and his plans are to prosper me and not harm me. His plans are to give me hope and a future. (Jeremiah 29:11).

As I prayerfully put this out there to the world, I pray that my story, in some small way, can be a catalyst for anyone ready to hand their own story over to the One who has plans for your future, to give you hope, and to bring you freedom.

CHAPTER ONE

Jesus Take the Pen

"Abide in me, and I in you. As the branch cannot bear
fruit by itself, unless it abides in the vine, neither can you,
unless you abide in me. I am the vine; you are the branches.
Whoever abides in me and I in him, he bears much fruit for
apart from me you can do nothing."
John 15: 4-5

"A machine can do work; only life can bear fruit. A law can
compel work; only love can spontaneously bring forth fruit.
Work implies effort and labor; the essential idea of fruit is
that it is the silent, natural, restful product of our inner life."
Andrew Murray, *The True Vine*
(https://www.goodreads.com/work/quotes/265033-the-true-vine)

ELLEN

Like yours, my story begins with those who came before me.

My parents were members of the "greatest generation." Every generation has its own strengths and weaknesses, a different prioritization of values, as well as its own blind spots.

My parents' strength lay in their tenacious work ethic. This formed in me the mindset "to always push or pull or strive a little harder." Their weakness was also in their tenacious work ethic. Work was what they valued most, often at the detriment of their own relationships, their own faith, and their kids.

Because of this, much of my life can be defined by the word "over" – overworking, over-extending, overthinking. As a result, I have often felt over-burdened. With a high value on performance, I was trained to seek the approval of others by over-functioning and over-accommodating.

Yet, no matter what I did, it never seemed like enough.

While I am deeply grateful for the strong work ethic my parents modeled, it blinded the eyes of my heart for years.

It likely still does in ways I have yet to uncover.

Difficulties certainly shaped my parent's stories.

One early memory I have is of overhearing my parents talking privately in their bedroom. I snuck quietly down the hall and put my ear to the door, curious about why my mom was crying and why my dad was so angry. Creeping near the closed door to their bedroom, I strained to hear what they were quietly discussing.

Something about losing all their savings.

More about my dad being talked into a bad deal.

I would find out years down the road that my dad's brother had persuaded him into investing most of his savings in a new company. Against his gut feelings, my dad chose to help his brother but with disastrous outcomes. The company went belly up and my dad lost his savings, which resulted in a *waste-nothing-spend-little plan* for our family.

As a result of this, when I was growing up, we often lived as if we were impoverished even though we weren't. We purchased little from the grocery store and instead filled our stomachs with canned or frozen produce from our land, eggs from our chickens and meat from a cow we butchered. We borrowed books from the mail order library. My mom made our clothes and cut our hair.

I am still amazed that my dad went to the grave never having owned a credit card, yet he left my mom and his five kids with a substantial inheritance..... and a legacy of resilient self-sufficiency.

My dad was ten when the great depression began, a downturn which lasted past World War II. In spite of difficult times, he managed to nearly complete an advanced medical degree, then enlisted to serve as a medic in the war. After the war, he changed course and completed a law degree instead.

He was highly intelligent, highly motivated, and highly educated. While he practiced law in our rural community, serving as the district and school board attorney, he also managed our 300-acre farm and a herd of cattle.

My mom was very different from my dad. She only had an 8th grade education, and before immigrating to the United States when she was 22, she knew only a handful of English words.

She grew up in Kalajoki, Finland, a tiny town in a small country that was ravaged by both the Nazis and the Russians during World War 2. My mom was one of eight children, and growing up, her entire life was focused on survival. She never worried about which dress to wear or which shoes to buy, but instead worried that she would have a dress. Or shoes. Or food.

My mom had struggled greatly as a child. And I am grateful for the strength and resolve that these difficulties carved into the character of my mom. After the war, they had little more than the land they lived on, and they learned to be very resourceful, using everything on their farm to survive. My mom told me about how a "suutari" or shoemaker would come to live in their home for a few weeks each year to make shoes for each family member from the dried hide of a cow they had butchered. The lard from that same cow was used to make soap. Vegetables and berries from their gardens were carefully stored in cold cellars for the long winter months. With extra milk, they made yogurt and cheese.

They had no electricity or running water. Bread was made from the wheat and rye grown on their own land and was baked fresh each week in a wood burning oven. They raised flax plants, weaving the linen into cloth for their clothing, sheets and even mattress covers. The dark winters were spent in candlelight, with the women knitting woolen socks, mittens, and hats for whoever needed them.

Because of this upbringing, my mom was full of "sisu", a word that defines the resilient mindset of the Finnish people. Sisu is about determination, courage, and tenacity all wrapped together, which rose out of the difficult circumstances her generation grew up under.

Both of my parents learned to survive through hard work and resourcefulness. It's easy to see why they both valued work so much.

My parents met in his law office in the rural community of Clatskanie, Oregon. My mom had just immigrated from Finland, and when she learned that the town attorney was also of Finnish descent, she went to him with hopes that he would sponsor her boyfriend who was interested in following her to Oregon.

Instead, my dad asked her out on a date and four months later they married.

The boyfriend was quickly forgotten.

These stories, as well as many others shaped my parents into the people they were: tenacious, hardworking, independent, motivated. Yet peace and contentment seemed to evade both of their hearts, making them both, at times, distant, harried and discontent.

This spilled over into my childhood home.

Later in life, when they both personally met Jesus, they changed.

My dad was very skeptical about faith for most of his life. He had managed difficulties and overcome obstacles well and he regarded reliance on God as a crutch. Yet as he grew older, his fierce individualism gave way to a deeper need in his heart. As his own strength began to wane at the end of his life, he began to see a need for something stronger outside of himself.

Likewise, my mom seemed to constantly face a deep unsettling discontentment, and only through prayer and dependence on Jesus did her soul seem to find rest.

Early in 2023, a severe storm blew into Austin, Texas where I live. In a city where temperatures rarely drop below freezing, freezing rain followed by icy cold wind created a layer of ice that blanketed every tree, shrub, and house in the area.

It devastated our trees.

For days, as the ice melted, we listened to loud pops and cracks as branch after branch fell around our city. Piles of limbs stacked up on the sides of streets, trees stood bare on the skyline, people were afraid to go outside.

It was surreal, and also unprecedented.

Arborists surmised that an equally unusual polar vortex snow storm in 2022 caused damage to the trees, then the subsequent drought the following summer damaged them more. These events piled up to cause disaster.

The city lost thousands and thousands of trees of trees.

Jesus refers to us as branches and himself as the vine.

If you're anything like me, that may not sound appealing to our modern ears. There have been times in my life when the idea of being a branch felt archaic and stifling. Instead, think about it in terms of the trees I talked about above. On their own, those trees were vulnerable, without hope when the ice came.

But when Jesus is our vine, we can depend on him.

He's protecting us from the ice and the wind.

He's standing guard against the drought.

Debi says that she pictures in her mind a healthy oak tree with many branches. When a storm comes with heavy winds, some branches will remain connected, while weak ones will fall off. Likewise, she says that she knows that a branch on a grape vine will not bear fruit unless connected to the vine. Jesus the vine and the source of our strength, makes us grow and remain healthy so that we can weather the storms that come. Those that turn away from him, rather than surrendering, grow weakened by anxiety, brokenness, and bad choices. Basically, we must always get our nourishment from the vine and not look in another direction.

The life of a branch is not a lazy restfulness but a deeper awareness of how to thrive by surrendering ourselves to dependence on the vine. In Andrew Murray's classic book, *Absolute Surrender*, he states that God has done everything for people to live productive, meaningful lives and believed that the obstacle for many was a resistance to surrender.

In Matthew 11:28-30, we see that Jesus made this sentiment clear:

> *"Come to me, all who labor and are heavy laden, and I will give you rest. Take my yoke upon you and learn from me; for I am gentle and lowly in heart, and you will find rest for your souls. For my yoke is easy and my burden is light."*

He wants to protect his branches.

Perhaps the feelings of heaviness that so many of us feel come from the burdens we place on our own hearts. Our anxious thinking. Our striving to write our own story.

He is more than able to write a much better story than we are.

Priscilla Shirer in her book, *Fervent,* wrote that if she were your enemy, she would *"work hard to ensure that you never realize what God has given you, so you'll doubt the power of God within."*

The devil's tactics haven't changed.

We want to let God write our stories, but instead, we are tempted to write our own.

As if we could do it better.

Later in life, my parents discovered that their own efforts fell short of meeting the deeper needs of their hearts. They were able to carve out success through hard work, but their own strength eventually ran out.

Like so many of us, they were never meant to write their own stories.

Instead, they were meant to give Jesus their pens.

When we abide in Christ, his words live in us, and he pours into us all we need to flourish. When he's writing our stories, we are healthy. We can withstand freezing rain, droughts, and yes, even polar vortexes. But when we are writing our own stories, we are vulnerable to pressure from unexpected events. When the icy winds come, when temperatures drop, when we find ourselves in the wilderness, we can't withstand the storm.

Life can feel like a series of storms. Both of my parents felt it, and I know you have too. These storms threaten to destroy everything dear to us. Weather events. Health issues. Relationship issues. Financial hardships.

Facing these trials, as James says, with joy, does not mean we have to pretend to be happy in the face of them. Trials are not joyous occasions. Rather, they are often painful and frightening, but we can joyfully anticipate what God will do in and through them. Storms are a means to strengthen us, not cause us to break and shrivel up to be discarded.

Revival blossoms out of brokenness when we allow Jesus to take the pen and start writing our stories.

CHAPTER TWO

Writing Resilience

"God is still writing your story.
Don't let go of your faith because of what you have yet to see."
Johnny R. Powell

"Tell the story of the mountain you climbed.
Your words could become a page in someone else's
survival guide."
Morgan Harper Nichols

My story was very different from my mom's or my dad's.

In my household, I never worried about an errant bomb or that I would have something to eat. I was never unsafe. I always had shoes and clothes. I was one of the few girls in my high school who got to go to college. Yet, I had very little when it came to supervision or mentorship or parental guidance.

During my grade school years, my parents would drop me and my siblings off at a small neighborhood country church each Sunday. They did not attend church themselves, but instead saw Sunday mornings as a welcome break from the chatter and clamor of five children. Although my parents were not believers and didn't raise me in a so-called "Christian home", God's Word was planted in my heart at an early age, thanks to caring and compassionate Sunday School teachers.

I had no Bible at home, but I played my favorite hymn, "In the Garden," over and over on the piano singing along with the music:

"I come to the garden alone, while the dew is still on the roses; and the voice I hear, falling on my ear, the Son of God discloses."

I felt a deep joy when I sang the refrain:

"And he walks with me, and he talks with me, and he tells me I am his own, and the joy we share as we tarry there, none other has ever known."

Singing this hymn calmed my soul as I pictured a God who saw me and knew me as his own.

Growing up in a large family, with parents who ran a farm and a law practice, I got very little attention from my parents. I did not feel seen or known. My parents knew little of what was going on inside of me, but somehow I knew God did. I had simple child-like faith but with age, my faith began to get complicated by life itself.

My core identity as a child formed around helping and supporting my siblings. I was the second oldest of five, with a mere four years separating all but our youngest brother. In their teen years, each of my brothers and sisters struggled in various ways, which heightened my own anxiety and desire to please. My oldest sister fell into the drug-infested commune scene of the late 60's. My younger sister became very anxious, clinging to me for stability. My 18-year-old brother married his 16-year-old pregnant girl-friend, Debi, who you can probably guess is now my closest friend and a contributor to this book. My youngest brother suffered from mental illness, causing him to struggle to manage every day task.

Not wanting to add to the tension in my family, I took on the role of helper and counselor to my siblings. Remember what I said about "over" doing everything? I went over the top in trying to stabilize things for them, trying to make sure they were okay, they didn't get hurt, they didn't get in trouble.

I worried about them constantly and carried their burdens in my heart much like a parent would. Because my parents focused on everything except their kids, I overfocused on my siblings.

My worth grew out of being needed by others, which set me up to become ensnared in an abusive relationship during high school. I wound up dating a manipulative guy who was five years older than me. He had graduated as a star athlete, who was revered by parents, teachers, and students alike. When he showed an interest in me, a freshman, I was pleasantly surprised.

I was also nervous.

My tendency to overthink and over-involve myself made me hesitant to enter any relationship, especially with someone who was much older than me.

The relationship was difficult from the start. Randy was controlling and harsh with me. He would pick me up each morning and drive me to school, a 30-minute ride, in his gold Camaro. This likely looked charming to others, but inside the car, I endured a half hour of berating every day about how I had dressed or what I had said. He threatened me if I talked to any other guys. He demeaned me for everything I said and did.

On the way home each day, I would be quizzed incessantly about the day. I remember a time when we stopped to get a soda on the way home. I must have smiled when I thanked the clerk, which was all it took to throw Randy into a rage. As we continued home that day, I argued back which resulted in my being shoved out of the car and left on the side of the road.

Yet in my mind, I justified this.

He was just overprotective.

He overreacted once but wouldn't do it again.

He was just trying to be a good boyfriend.

In reality, I was terrified of him.

I was also terrified of telling anyone how I felt, too afraid I would disappoint someone.

My parents never did find out that their daughter was under the thumb of a controlling, jealous, anger-ridden dangerous man. I occasionally hinted as to what was happening, but they were too busy and wrapped in their own world to notice.

So I just "toughed" it out.

I tried to break up with Randy several times, but he would threaten and then convince me that it was my duty to stay on as his girlfriend. When he enlisted that year, I made the mental decision to just stick with it until he was deployed. I counted the days until he had to report to duty.

I was immensely relieved when he left for Vietnam.

But my "tough it out" plan quickly backfired. He got injured in the war and was sent home to recover. Any guesses as to who was the first person he called when he returned?

In hindsight, I wish I would have not kept this part of my life hidden from my parents and friends. I did not feel safe because I wasn't safe. Yet I was afraid to share as my fear of disappointing others was greater than my fear for my own safety. Lies from the enemy of my soul turned these secrets into shame, deceiving me into thinking I had brought all the mistreatment onto myself and that I somehow deserved it.

And so the abuse continued.

My last year of high school was shrouded in this fear and deception. He was home from the war, living in our small town expecting his "girlfriend" to be there for him while controlling every move I made.

I rationalized it, telling myself that I loved him. That all relationships have problems. That his behavior was normal in relationships.

Overthinking. Overanxious. Overwhelmed.

That was the story I wrote for myself in childhood.

I told myself that if I just did more, *was* more, that I would be loved and cared for. And so I did everything I could to go above and beyond. I overdid it. I did everything, yet I felt like nothing.

In all that nothing, God was there.

He was there in the hymns that I sang at home while playing the piano.

He was there in the words of my Sunday school teachers.

He was there in the prayers of my grandparents far away in Finland.

He was there.

And he was writing.

CHAPTER THREE

Writing Faith

"Because of the tender mercy of our God,
whereby the sunrise shall visit us from on
high to give light to those who sit in darkness and in the
shadow of death,
to guide our feet into the way of peace."
Luke 1: 78-79

"Every path is a journey to God. We just have to remember to
open our hearts again and again".
Jeff Brown, author

I first met my sister-in-law Debi when she was 16 years old. She walked into my house wearing short shorts (we called hot pants back then) and white go-go boots. My younger brother Matt introduced her as his new girlfriend.

There was something about her that I immediately liked. She had a warm smile and joyful presence, and she seemed genuinely interested in me and my family.

At that time, my brother was already struggling. He was partying hard and spending more time hanging out with friends than studying. So it was not a huge surprise to anyone when a year later, a pregnant teenage Debi would walk down the aisle with my brother.

I would have been surprised to know that Debi would become one of my closest friends. As you've likely guessed, she's still one of my closest friends. In the past 50 (yes, 5-0) years, I have learned more and more about the story God has written for Debi. It is implicitly intertwined with my own, and yet distinctly unique to her.

One thing is certain: Debi's story is still being written by God. He has refined her, renewed her, and revealed himself to her through it all. And through that "writing", despite big setbacks and lots of pain, Debi's story is one of resilience, encouragement, and inspiration as to what can happen when someone truly gives themselves over to God's story.

DEBI

"Please don't let this happen," I prayed silently to a God I didn't yet believe existed. But even before the doctor entered the room, before he told me the news, I knew it was true.

I was pregnant.

Sixteen years old and pregnant.

It's funny, because for my entire childhood I had longed for *family*. For connection. My dad had abandoned my family for another woman, and having experienced that instability and abandonment, I desperately wanted to be loved and valued. This deep longing had led me to give myself fully to a handsome teen, the son of the town attorney, who had set his eyes on me. Matt's affection gave me hope.

But now that I had a chance at family– although with imperfect circumstances - I was absolutely terrified. How could I manage a baby? How would I feed it? How would I tell my parents? How would I finish school?

But then, new thoughts came. A baby would be family. He or she would love me no matter what. It felt like a world of love could be opening up to me. It was almost my chance to step out of the life I knew, and into one with hope. Maybe this baby was everything I had been hoping for.

My childhood was rocky.

My dad was a truck driver by trade and jobs were scarce at times. When work dried up, we would move to a new location. Because of that, I lived in countless small towns and cities as a child.

Due to many health issues, my mom did not work. Suffering with a blood disorder, depression, anxiety, and poor vision, she struggled to care for her three children. One day, I heard my mom crying on the phone to my dad, *"Please come back to me!"* He was out of town on another job and that was the day we learned of his infidelity. He did come back and stayed for a while, but later, he decided to leave us for good when family life became too complicated for him.

A short while after that phone call, my mom was hit by a drunk driver, which resulted in ongoing chronic back pain and a lasting addiction to pain medication. At times, she would grow extremely irrational, and on occasion, was even committed to the state mental hospital for extended periods of time.

My entire childhood was full of these little traumas that added up to a constant feeling of instability and fear of abandonment. One of my earliest memories was of a neighbor who, thinking it would be funny to scare a young girl, lunged through our front door in a monster costume and raised a club at me. Another memory was of the ruckus caused when a convicted criminal tried to break into our home via the back door where the sheriff finally caught up with him.

When I was eleven, a murder took place in the apartments next door. The FBI came and took residence in our home for a few days until they caught the murderer in the alley outside my bedroom window. I also remember the day when my sister was severely attacked by her husband who threw her small dog against the wall as he attempted to strangle her. This resulted in a miscarriage later that evening.

These are just flashes of memories from my childhood– things that I remember happening almost as if they were normal, typical. I had no idea that these kinds of things didn't happen to other kids in other families.

Like Matt and Ellen, I didn't grow up in a Christian home, yet even as a child, I also remember moments when I felt God speaking to me. For a short while, we lived near a pastor's family and their daughter became my best friend. On their property was a prayer barn that always had a strong, woodsy odor. One day I asked God, *"If you're real, make the smell of this place change."* Walking into the barn, I was surprised and amazed that the smell had remarkably changed. Now a more pleasant odor permeated the room, a moment in time that had a lasting effect on me.

I now know that even though I didn't know him, he was already writing my story.

With all this tumult, I remember feeling unaccepted as a child. My brother and sister were quiet introverts and fit in better with extended family, but my dad's side of the family didn't have much tolerance for my boisterous personality. So I remember feeling like an outsider, yet wanting to be on the inside, especially when I was scared, or things got unstable.

As soon as I met Matt, I was smitten. He loved my energy and accepted me for who I was. He made me feel valued and loved.

I was three months pregnant and close to completing my junior year when Matt and I got married. He was almost nineteen and promised to care for me and our baby and that was all I needed to say an exuberant yes when he proposed.

Together, we moved into a small apartment and came face-to-face with the challenges and responsibilities of adult life. Not only were we figuring out how to be married, but we had to figure out how to pay our bills, how to cook meals, and how to keep our apartment tidy.

Six months later, Angie was born, and I was thrilled. For the first time in my life, I was hopeful. My daughter was beautiful. My husband loved me. I had a family.

At that point, I still had a semester of high school to finish. I honestly was so caught up in school and managing my house that I hardly considered how to parent, but I do remember wondering if I should add a religious element into my child's life. It seemed like the right thing to do, and since I wanted my daughter to have all of the security and hope I had never had.

Also, with all the changes in my life, I was growing more curious about spiritual matters. One day, seeing the steeple of a church from the window of our apartment, I thought, *"Now that we have a daughter, perhaps it's time to start going to church."*

I thought about it. But never quite followed through.

After I graduated from high school, we decided that Matt should go to college and get a degree. While he went to school, I took the night shift as a waitress to make ends meet. His college years proved to be a very difficult season for me. Matt did really well in class, enjoyed college life, and even got connected with a Christian group.

He was changing and growing and making friends… all while I was working various shifts and taking care of Angie. I was exhausted and lonely. I was tired and worn out. Meanwhile, Matt was anything but. He was excited about what he was learning, but because we never had time to talk, we no longer shared the closeness we had in our first months of marriage.

We began to argue. A lot.

Then, one day, he came home from class and announced that he had become a Christian. Honestly, I silently balked at his faith. I didn't understand it, and I certainly didn't want it to drive us further apart. So I agreed to join him at the local Baptist church.

I began to accompany Matt on Sundays, partly out of curiosity but mostly out of fear that he was leaving me behind. Each Sunday, sitting in the back, I felt a war taking place within me. God would whisper, *"go forward for the altar call,"* and Satan would yell, *"you don't want to walk down that long aisle."*

This took place for weeks. Maybe even months.

The Holy Spirit began to nudge me during the week as well. One day, while cooking spaghetti, with baby Angie nearby in a highchair, I decided to call the pastor and ask him the questions that were burning in me. After dialing his number, however, fear took over and I hung up. I returned to the pot of spaghetti sauce only to hear the doorbell ring. Standing at the door was our pastor! God had told him to pay me a visit.

That day, with tears of relief, I gave my life to the Lord.

Shortly afterwards, Matt walked through the door and was able to pray as a family with our pastor.

I have never regretted the decision I made that day.

My newfound faith did not change everything overnight, but the light of Christ was now burning within me, and I began to see everything through a different lens. Matt and I attended a couple's Bible study together, and while we were growing closer, life continued to include traumatic events..

A few months after I found Christ, Angie fell off of our third story apartment balcony. I didn't hear her fall but, somehow, knew that she had. I raced down the stairs and around the corner to the back of the apartments to find my 18-month-old daughter lying eerily still on the sidewalk. Gathering my limp, unresponsive baby up into my arms, I ran to the neighbor who drove us to the closest hospital where we spent the next several days. I remained oddly calm even when the doctors expressed grave concerns over potentially permanent brain damage. God's presence carried me graciously through this ordeal, and I was so grateful that I had found him before it happened.

Thankfully, Angie made a full recovery, and Matt and I went back to our lives as young parents.

ELLEN

Debi's hunger for love and acceptance may have been exacerbated by a childhood full of abandonment but the truth is her hunger came from God. God created each of us with a heart that longs to love and hunger for something greater and stronger and wiser.

This longing is what drives each of us, like Debi did, to search for meaning in our lives. Jesus addressed this core longing in John 1:38 when he turned and asked two of his disciples who were following him, "*What are you seeking?*"

The loves of our heart reflect what we value and fervently seek after our idols. "This is the most incisive, piercing question Jesus can ask of us," wrote James K.A. Smith in *You are What You Love*. "What is at the core of the human person is found not in the intellect but in the love of the heart at its gut-level." Every decision we make, every action we take, flows out of our deepest wants and needs.

Idols are strongholds the enemy has gained in our lives that we need freedom from. This begins with a choice to allow Christ to occupy our hearts instead and free us from our own internal bondage.

For Debi, this led her to seek love and acceptance from a man.

For others, that idol may be money, power, fame, success, alcohol, drugs, or any of hundreds of other things. I've even known people who have idolized exercising. Imagine that!

The Israelites fell into idol worship over and over despite all that God did for them. Samuel implored the Israelites saying, *"Do not turn aside after empty things that cannot profit or deliver, for they are empty."* (I Samuel 12: 21) Idols in our hearts fuel anxiety because they lead us away from what can meet our deepest longings. Even so, I easily fall back into seeking after empty things: Approval from others. Affirmation. Comfort. Any desire that consumes me more than my love for God is an idol.

God's Word exposes what these are. *"For the word of God is living and active, sharper than any two-edged sword, piercing to the division of soul and of spirit, of joints and of marrow, and discerning the thoughts and intentions of the heart."* (Hebrews 4:12)

When the loves of my heart are rightly ordered, my heart grows calm and free. Therefore, I must willingly put myself under the microscope of God's Word, to reveal and root out any intentions that do not honor him as the highest priority of my heart.

We can know a lot about God and still have a heart that is far from him. Likewise, we can know a lot about others but fail to love them well. We each have a tendency to find ways to meet the need of intimacy, but unless we find intimacy with the Lord, we will never meet that need. When we allow his presence to heal hurt, and reveal deception, we can love with a free heart.

CHAPTER FOUR

Writing Truth

"I know, O Lord, that the way of man is not in himself,
that it is not in man who walks to direct his steps".
Jeremiah 10:23

"He reveals deep and hidden things; he knows what is in the darkness,
and the light dwells with him."
Daniel 2:22

ELLEN

I finally graduated high school.

I was still with Randy, but while he hung around our small town in Oregon doing odd jobs, I had been admitted into a fairly prestigious university a few hours away. I was the only girl in my graduating class who had even applied to college, and there was no way, no how I was going to let that opportunity pass me by.

I made promises to Randy that we would be fine long-distance, that we would make it work, that I would be loyal to him. But I knew college was my escape, my way to break off the relationship.

I was ready, even if part of me wondered if I ever would truly escape.

From day one in college, I covered up deep seated feelings of shame and unworthiness, never letting on that I was struggling and scared. Secrecy formed another layer of deception and anxiety around my heart.

I was terrified of Randy, yet afraid to break it off with him.

One afternoon, he came to the college I lived at, but I refused to come out of the all-women's dorm. That was the day he stopped pursuing me.

I lacked the skills to set boundaries or say no. I found it easier to say and do what others wanted. Because of this tendency, needy people seemed to sniff me out. Away from Randy and my siblings, I still managed to become the constant caregiver and counselor to many.

I can't put all the blame on others for me not having support because I rarely let on that I needed any. I craved the feeling of being needed, and so I drew close to people who, well, needed me. Anyone who needed a friend to talk to, a shoulder to lean on, someone to help with their laundry, or someone to tutor them, I was there.

My roommate got jealous if I spent time with other friends, so I hung out in the dorm with her even when invited to go bowling or to a school event.

Another friend had a rocky relationship with her boyfriend, so I spent hours listening, never telling her a word about myself.

Now looking back, it's clear that the story I had written for myself was all about what I could do. I had defined myself as a caregiver, a listener, a friend, a supporter and had never allowed God to work in me and help me to figure out *who* I was at my core.

My soul, my very being, had been taken over by a story that wasn't true.

The word "soul" comes from the Greek word "psyche" and refers to one's inward being, the very breath of life within.

I don't *have* a soul. I *am* a soul.

When the breath of Jesus fills my soul, I become a new creature. My soul is the deepest part of who I am. Seeing myself as God sees me is the means to emotional and spiritual wholeness.

Our souls have great receptive capacities. They are always receiving input, from the world, from people, from our experiences, from our past. These inputs shape us to our very core, demonstrating how essential it is for us to monitor what input our soul receives.

Do we want God to be our main source of input? Or others, the world, and our experiences?

The answer should be obvious, but in case it isn't, the answer is God. Input influences our souls. So do our experiences and how we remember them. At our core, we must allow God's presence to shape us. Not others. Not the input from the world. Not ourselves. Not even our experiences. We love God best when we love him as the person that he created us to be – not the ones we try to be, or want to be, or attempt to change ourselves into. Sin, pride, brokenness and disappointment can distort the input our souls receive how we see ourselves, but God speaks to our true identities.

He writes our true stories.

Perhaps those times, when God feels distant (like I often felt in the middle of college), are the times when we are unable to hear him because we are trapped within a false sense of self.

Satan wants to fill our minds with lies so that we grow blind to who we are and to the power God has given us. He connives ways in which we see ourselves falsely because he knows we will fall into despair when we walk in a false sense of self. He doesn't want us reading God's Word or praying because both reveal our true identities. The Bible tells us that while we formerly walked in darkness, we are now children of light, able through Christ to be lights in the world. (Ephesians 5:8-9) Our identity is one of light and not darkness. We are children of the day. (I Thessalonians 5:4)

Satan's lies, which he often shrouds in partial truth, cause us to wear false labels. For example, If I fall for the lie that I am defined by how I perform (which is a lie I have fallen for often in my life), then it's an "all up to me" kind of striving that produces anxiety.

Yet, in a real sense, there's always something more that I could have, should have, or will need to do, and I end up questioning my way through life. If I see myself as someone who is rejected, I begin to act rejected. Having experienced real rejection, trusting again will feel risky.

That's exactly the story I wrote for myself in college.

I had been so hurt by Randy, and seemingly unnoticed by my parents, and in turn, I became someone who was constantly striving for acceptance. As Benjamin Franklin said, "*The things you do often create the things you believe.*"

True stories come from true beliefs. And true beliefs come from the only One who *is* true.

My own story reflected this for years. The harder I tried to do all and be all for others, the more anxious I grew. The more anxious I grew, the more I believed that my only value was in how I could support and care for others.

My soul believed a lie.

I was trusting my own efforts, my own input, not God's..

I was writing my own story.

Jesus is our king who has invited us to walk closely with him. "*No longer do I call you servants, for a servant does not know what his master is doing, but I have called you friends, for all that I have heard from my father, I have made known to you.*" (John 15:15)

Jesus meets our deepest needs, heals our wounds, and calls us his beloved as he writes our stories, and he shows us how to walk in freedom as he does it.

Satan is after our souls. But so is God.

As I traversed college, with few people who truly knew me, I allowed my soul to be shaped by my own preconceptions, my own anxiety, and by others.

I needed to allow God to *be* the input that shaped my story.

In his inspirational book, *Living Fearless*, Jamie Winship lays out a simple process by which to gain a God-breathed identity. He explains that clarity will come when we ask God for it. Through this process, we can ask him to reveal false identities that have taken root in our soul and to define us according to his creative purpose in each of us. We have not because we ask not. Undoubtedly, God wants us to know who he has created us to become, so:

- Ask God what he wants you to know about yourself.

- Then sit in silence and listen.

- Wait. Be still and know that he is God. (Psalm 46:10). He knit you together in your mother's womb. (Psalm 139) He knows your giftings and your weaknesses. He created you for good works so that you would walk in them. (Ephesians 2:10)

- Write down what he quietly says about who you are.

This process feels vulnerable. Uncomfortable even.

I'm not certain I could have managed to do it back in college, but as I've grown, I've learned that the only way to know his story for my life is to allow him to speak to me.

What God says about you will never contradict scripture.

It will never be untrue nor accusatory.

It will never be based on false inputs or lies from Satan.

When I recently went through this process, I heard the Lord call me "*a mouthpiece for hope in him.*" While it felt weird to claim this, it resonated deeply because my heart's cry for others has always been about keeping hope alive. A close friend, who I often turn to for counsel, heard the Lord called her "*a gentle truth teller.*" And she is just that!

My sister-in-law Debi, who helped me write this book and shared her own story a chapter back, told me that God called her a *faithful encourager*. And that's true about her. Encouragement is a spiritual gift that comes so easily to her, and I have seen that since she was young. She told me that she constantly wants to give others hope for the future, to keep going on and not give up, that they are not alone.

Yet she also told me something interesting: She said that at the times when she was walking on her own, when she was writing her own story, encouragement didn't come as easily to her. Instead, it was when she pressed into God and let him write her story that her heart grew compassionate toward those who are suffering, and she felt a desire to ease their pain.

Easing another's pain makes her feel fulfilled.

Yet when God isn't writing her story, she doesn't feel compelled to be the *faithful encourager* that she is.

When we know who we are in Christ, when he is writing our story, then the person we truly are is there.

We can patiently bear annoyances and not grow angry over insults.

We can be overlooked and unnoticed without growing hurt.

We can remain joyful in struggle while friends prosper.

When he is writing our story, we can stay calm and trusting regardless of the circumstances we are in.

When He is writing our story, we find hope and joy knowing that *"we are his workmanship, created in Christ Jesus for good works, which God prepared beforehand, that we should walk in them."* (Ephesians 2:10)

There is deep peace in understanding the value God has assigned each of us. While we are imperfect and prone towards making mistakes, we are still wonderfully and uniquely made. We are so valuable to God that he calls us by name. Our worth lies in our creation – in our Imago Dei. So, ask him. Listen.

CHAPTER FIVE

Writing Healing

Jesus answered, "The most important is, 'Hear, O Israel: The Lord our God, the Lord is one. And you shall love the Lord your God with all your heart and with all your soul and with all your mind and with all your strength.' The second is this: 'You shall love your neighbor as yourself.' There is no other commandment greater than these."
Mark 12: 29-31

"But for you who fear my name, the sun of righteousness shall rise with healing in its wings You shall go out leaping like calves from the stall."
Malachi 4:2

 ELLEN

Throughout college, I grew in so many ways.

I did well in school. I joined a sorority. I was a cheerleader for the football team.

Yet, I still struggled with that old tendency to go "over". I still went overboard helping people and still stifled my own feelings and needs at the expense of others. I also still tended to overwork and overthink, almost as a defense mechanism to stay out of my own head.

At the start of my senior year, a guy named Dave asked me out. I went, and we had a good time, so we made plans to go out again.

At the same time, I started attending an encounter group set up by my psychology professor. This professor, Dr. Bumpus, taught my senior level Psych courses and encouraged us all to form encounter groups in which to discuss the Bible. (unlike the other professors in this very liberal department!)

Another student named Glen also attended the very same encounter group.

I had gone to school with Glen for several years, but we had never really gotten to know each other. But that fall, we started talking.

We became good friends.

My sort-of boyfriend Dave didn't like that.

It turns out that old wounds tend to resurface as time goes on. When Dave got jealous of my friendship with Glen, I had immediate flashbacks to Randy. I panicked. I thought back to the controlling, overly intense relationship that I had managed to escape and realized that Dave and I would never work.

I broke it off with him.

And that's when I started thinking about Glen in a different way.

Glen was everything that my previous boyfriends weren't. He was steady, he was calm, and he wasn't jealous at all. We were able to talk and share about our lives.

What's more, Glen's family seemed like my dream family. He told me about his mom and how she cooked him four homemade meals a day. She had a full meal ready for her boys each day when they got home from school. His family traveled together. They ate together. They laughed together.

Glen's vision for the future seemed exactly like mine: Family, faith, kids, a future.

We started dating in November and were married the next November.

God was writing healing into my story.

When wounds in our hearts are left unaddressed and unhealed, we will relate with others in broken, self-protective ways. Looking back on my college years, and especially my early dating relationships, I realize how much damage Randy caused.

Randy made me fearful and protective.

It took someone new, someone different, someone with God's heart in mind for me to find that healing.

I entered our marriage longing for affirmation having grown up in a home in which little was given. What I didn't realize at the time was that Glen had grown up with a father who was quick to criticize and slow to affirm.

He had his own healing to do. As we all do.

In those early years of marriage, my desire for affirmation and Glen's pattern of criticism collided. I began to erect "protective" layers around my heart, and the more I closed myself up, the more critical and frustrated Glen became.

He longed for a wife who would engage with him.

I longed for emotional safety in my marriage.

We began to disconnect ourselves from each other and wound up in a long season when we rarely spoke. I was living with an impaired heart, stuffing my emotions, and blocking relational efforts because of fear. I would defend myself from potential pain, by choosing not to be vulnerable or authentic.

I was aware of my own pain but not of Glen's.

He was aware of his pain but not mine.

The walls we built between ourselves gave us a false sense of control, yet with distant hearts, we grew distrustful and cynical of each other. All the while, God was quietly urging me to open my heart again by stepping out from behind the walls. As I laid myself bare before God, the courage to be honest with Glen began to take hold as well. God intervened and began to break down our defenses.

He began to write the story of our marriage.

And his story set us free to seek out a healthy marriage.

Feelings are how our hearts speak, central to every aspect of our lives. A wide range of opinions exist regarding emotions that flow from the heart. On the one hand we are told that our emotions are irrational or a sign of weakness – that they are to be suppressed. Yet the Bible is full of the out-pouring of emotions:

- Psalm 6:6 – "*I am weary with my moaning, every night I flood my bed with tears.*"

- Matthew 27: 46 "*My God, my God, why have you forsaken me?*"

- Acts 21:13- "*Paul answered, 'What are you doing weeping and breaking my heart?'*"

On the other hand, we are encouraged to not consider emotions to be the basis for everything. Yet just because they are real does not mean they reflect what is true. Our emotions cannot be used to determine what we believe, nor can our emotional experiences be used as the test for truth. We need God's truth, which is always real, to be the lens through which we examine our fears, our worries, and our loves. We are to trust the Lord with all of our heart and not trust in our own understanding. (Proverbs 3:5)

We are all broken people, prone to hurting one another, yet despite what others might do to us, we can be secure in the Lord. Openness is worth the risk when we place ourselves in his loving arms. This is how we allow God to write the stories of our relationships—relationships that are tender and sensitive, even if they hurt deeply at times. *"Tenderness, the opposite of that which is stout, obstinate, cold, hard, is one of the most gracious signs in a man's character,"* said Charles Spurgeon in his sermon on August 31, 1872.

We were made to be known by God. We were made to be known by others. To let our walls down feels risky. Vulnerable. But it's how we will experience true freedom and peace. We have a choice. We can seek answers in our own stories, written within the walls we erect around our hearts. Or we can choose to step outside these walls and give Jesus the pen.

This is where we grow and find fulfillment in our relationship with God and with others.

When I am willing to be honest with God, even about emotions I prefer to keep hidden, His love washes over me, and my heart grows restful and free. Chip Dodd describes this so beautifully on Pg. 139 of his book *The Voice of the Heart*:

> *"When the wall around our hearts is broken down, we are set free to experience and choose full living. We are needy, dependent, creatures who need to surrender our hearts so that we can experience how we are made – to be in relationship with ourselves, others, and especially God. When we do this daily, we begin to experience life through the heart, and we begin to experience the heart of God. We recognize that while life is often depressing, frustrating, and frightening, it is also wonderful, magnificent, and glorious."*

Chip Dodd goes on to describe what he calls the core feelings that all humans experience. These include feelings I would have considered "bad" until he explained how even these emotions are essential in allowing us to live fully and freely. He writes, *"Feelings are the voice of the heart, and you will not have fullness until you're adept at hearing and experiencing all of them."* He explains how we find deeper faith and greater strength when we live in total awareness of our heart's capacity to experience all emotions. Feeling emotional pain is not a sign that our faith is weak.

It takes courage to face brokenness and pain, but this is the way to healing and wholeness. The Lord is *"near to the broken-hearted and saves the crushed in spirit."* (Psalm 34:18)

Sometimes our emotions are the source of deep joy and well-being.

At other times they fill us with anxiety and despair. We grow upset with ourselves for being angry or sad because we tend to think of our feelings as the problems themselves, so we attempt to quiet them down.

As hard as I attempt to stuff them, as I often did in those early days of my marriage, these feelings will sometimes seep out through my broken places and even flood onto those around me. Rather than stuff, I can honestly express every single emotion to God in prayer and allow the Holy Spirit to guide and show me how to respond. He can change my grief into joy, my fear into courage, and my anger into compassion. He moves me away from self-serving introspection to genuine concern for others. When I go at it alone, I am prone to thoughts about how everything affects me. Dwelling too long on why I am sad or angry, or what has me afraid, can give these emotions a deeper hold on my heart. We were made to be outward focused towards others and not overly consumed with ourselves.

It took my relationship with Glen for me to allow God to write my story of healing.

It also took the pain of misunderstanding my own story to bring that healing.

In the *Voice of the Heart,* Chip Dobb writes, *"God created you and me as emotional and spiritual creatures — created to live fully in relationship with ourselves, with others, and with God. We are image bearers of God, actually stamped in our hearts with a hunger to live fully."* (pg.9)

Jesus's greatest commandment holds the most important keys to how we are to live fully. We are to love God with our heart, soul, mind, and strength all working together in harmony.

We are to allow him to write our story.

To trust him to write our story.

And to willingly concede our story of healing to him.

No amount of counseling – no self-help tips or personal improvement ideas – no amount of striving and working harder will address the anxiety a fractured self feels. Only in Jesus will we be made whole and fully alive. Without Jesus we are broken people with layers of inconsistent character, yet in his light, we are being perfected in love. (I John 4:18)

The word "perfect" comes from the Greek word *teleious* meaning wholeness – or living an integrated life with our actions aligning with his values and beliefs. We are complex human beings, created by God in intricate ways. The aim of life is to glorify God with our thinking, our words, our attitudes, and our actions – to be people of his presence who radiate his light and love to a hurting world.

This is how we thrive in his story.

This is how we find healing.

And this is how we are set free.

49

CHAPTER SIX

Writing an Escape

"For God, who said, 'Let light shine out of darkness,'
has shone in our hearts to give the light of the knowledge of
the glory of God in the face of Jesus Christ."
2 Corinthians 4:6

"I am the light of the world.
Whoever follows me will not walk in darkness,
but will have the light of life."
John 8:12

Just as I was finding healing as God wrote my story of a healthy marriage, my sister-in-law Debi was also finding healing.

Only recently did Debi reveal to me all the details about her very troubled childhood. I obviously knew about Debi's teenage pregnancy, and her love for my brother, but before she shared her story, I had assumed that my cheerful, tenderhearted sister-in-law had a fairly typical upbringing.

But her story is anything but typical.

Many people, when faced with the pain and trials she faced would have clung tightly to any semblance of security they had, would have relied on writing their own story, hoping that somehow they could find a glimmer of hope.

But not Debi.

Debi's story is one of continued healing as she gains understanding and wisdom from the influence of her past that God has redeemed her from. Her story demonstrates how our good God creates beauty out of ashes, gladness out of mourning and praise out of a faint spirit. (Isaiah 61: 3) God took the story of a pregnant teen with a rocky childhood and changed it into a story of thriving despite big odds, of resilience despite setbacks, and of encouragement for anyone who has faced a season of darkness, a season in the wilderness.

The Bible is full of people who faced long wilderness seasons when God's people wondered, "*Where are you God?*" I think of Sarah and Abraham. Jonah. Job. Moses. Like them we are tempted to move through the wilderness on our own instead of letting God do the work. Like these men and women in the Bible, we may not see his plans working out, but he is at work even when we are in the wilderness. Revival comes after the wilderness, not as we walk through it.

Similarly, we have all faced our own wilderness seasons.

We've all struggled.

We've all felt trapped, confused, marginalized, desperate, alone, and dissatisfied.

Yet now, looking back, we see how God has used that wilderness to set us free.

God's writing an escape story for each of us.

A way for us to escape the pain of our pasts and find freedom and peace and healing in the present.

He's doing it for me, just like he wrote one for Debi.

I never look back on my pregnancy or the time when Angie was a baby as a dark time.

Many teen moms may see an unplanned pregnancy as a mistake, or a problem, or as something that destroys their plans or their future. But not me. Because even then, I saw Matt as my future.

If I'm looking back at my wandering-in-the-wilderness seasons, that wasn't one of them. Almost immediately, the pregnancy seemed like a blessing.

Now I'm not saying it wasn't hard. My plans did change. While I wasn't really planning on going to college, I definitely wanted to finish high school and Angie's birth in December of my senior year made that hard.

I also wanted to gain some financial security, and having to care for a baby while my husband went to school, and I worked as a waitress at night wasn't exactly financially lucrative.

Times were hard.

But they were also good. God used my pregnancy and our hasty marriage as a way to bring me healing and hope.

God started writing my comeback.

As you remember, right after I got married, both Matt and I found God. While that didn't change everything overnight, for the first time in my life, I had security and stability and the affection that I so desperately craved.

My story was at almost a high point.

Matt graduated and settled into a well-compensated technology career.

Our son, Jeff, was born when Angie was four.

We purchased a home, enrolled our kids in school and activities, and became very involved in church.

We were a thriving middle-class Christian family.

I had made my comeback.

My dream of a family to love had become a reality. My kids were thriving. I had food in the fridge. We had clothes in our closets. I made dinner and chocolate chip cookies and made meals for neighbors in need.

I made it.

Yet even in my season of comeback, anxiety remained a regular companion the source of which remained a mystery to me. I tried therapy. Christian counseling. Medications. Prayer. I tried changing my thinking. I tried trying harder. Yet anxieties continued to darken my days and attack my hope.

As I created my own family story, I did my best to view my upbringing through rose-colored lenses. I did my best to stuff it aside, to forget the past, to focus on the present. After all, I was now a new person in Christ and my old life had no hold on me.

Or did it?

Was my present story still being construed through the lens of my past? Was my fear of catastrophes somehow related to trauma in my younger years? And why did I avoid conflict at any cost, often to my own detriment?

Today God is showing me how to connect the dots on the unfolding story of my life.

Before, I was doing my best to help God write my comeback. But now, I have given him the pen.

Now he's helping me write my way out of the wilderness.

My prior experiences left marks on my soul and every chapter afterwards has continued to shape me. All the way through, God has been patiently and tenderly etching his character into my being. I don't look back on these experiences with regret or anger. I look back with relief and gratitude as I see that God has been with me always, even before I acknowledged his existence.

God is changing the imaginations of my heart from anxiety to ones that flow from a living hope knowing my true inheritance is not earthly but imperishable. (I Peter 1:3-4) While my past has shaped me, I move forward with Christ who breathes fresh life into my soul, renews my strength, and sets me free. I am a child of the light, adopted by God and made pure by his grace. God has transformed my life from ashes to beauty and is repairing the ruins of generations.

Misery and darkness did not win in my life.

I may have wandered in the wilderness, but I never got lost.

God always wrote an escape plan.

Instead, every chapter has gathered more blessings, making the ugly parts fade away. "*Write bad things that are done to you in sand,* says an old proverb, "*and write the good things that happen to you on a piece of marble.*"

ELLEN

Jesus declared himself to be the light of the world.

Light has always been a symbol of his truth and presence, of wisdom and understanding. "*By a pillar of cloud, you led them in the day,*" declared Ezra in Nehemiah 9: 12, "*and by a pillar of fire in the night to light for them the way in which they should go."* John came to bear witness to Jesus and declared that *"In him was life, and the life was the light of men."* (John 1:4). Light is what it is- bright! Light dispels darkness. Light is his very presence which enables us to see what we are doing and where we are going.

How profound and glorious that we carry within us the very light of Christ!

Many of the earliest cultures viewed the sun, moon, and stars as deities. The ancient Romans revered their gods as true light. Even the emperor of Rome was seen as a divine light to worship while the Gnostics regarded the human soul as light. Essentially, they all exchanged light for God and worshiped the created rather than the Creator. *"Claiming to be wise, they became fools, and exchanged the glory of the immortal god for images...."* (Romans 1:22-23) Even though God revealed himself as light to the Israelites, he warned them not to worship or bow down to the sun, moon, and stars, (Deuteronomy 4:19) knowing that the pagan culture they lived in had shoplifted light as an object to be worshiped.

The New Testament writers certainly understood the challenge of recapturing the true meaning of light when they proclaimed, "God is light."

Light has always been revered. Einstein could see no end to his discoveries with light, stating *"for the rest of my life, I will reflect on what is light."* The very first thing God spoke into existence was light and God's creation continues to radiate gloriously in a multitude of ways.

Sunlight and rain produce awe-inspiring rainbows.

Bright skies turn shimmering lake waters into beautiful shades of blue.

The sun's ultraviolet rays convert proteins in our skin to Vitamin D3, which helps keep our immune systems strong.

Research reported in the National Library of Medicine indicates that a strong relationship exists between sunshine and the production of serotonin, which affects our moods, emotions and even our digestion.

Medicinally, light is both healing and restorative. Bright light therapy is used for mood disorders. Phototherapy is used for neonatal jaundice. Blue light is used for antimicrobial treatments. Laser light can both destroy tissue and deliver energy to tissue. It's considered to be a bloodless knife.

No wonder so many people from the dawn of time have been obsessed with light.

As a young girl, growing up in Western Oregon, the sun would disappear behind the clouds for days. When it finally broke through, I would sing for joy! Everything around me seemed brighter.

When the sun finally revealed itself after a long dreary spell, I would skip through my family's farm fields, pondering the unknowns of the universe. Seeing the sun invoked deep questions in me. *What does eternity mean? And how big is the universe? How can God take care of everyone on earth? Does He really notice me?*

Pondering these mysteries not only filled me with awe, but also overwhelmed me as I struggled to comprehend an incomprehensible God! As time went on, I gained a simple concept of faith. We didn't talk much about God at home, but in Sunday School I learned that salvation came by asking Jesus into my heart and believing that he died for me. So, one day I prayed a simple prayer asking Jesus to save me, and immediately a light began to flicker within.

That faith that began in childhood is still growing today, layer by layer God is accomplishing his work in me. Jesus is breaking through my strongholds. He is shining through the shadows. He is light and life to me.

He is writing about my escape.

My mother came to faith in her mid 40's in the same small country church where I met Jesus. As a result, deep changes began to take hold in her heart as well. Rather than running around frantically every moment of the day to accomplish all she had to do, she would spend increasing time on her knees in prayer. I watched her vivacious, strong-willed spirit take on a gentler side and her anxious mindset begin to grow calmer.

Sadly, she was afflicted with Alzheimer's Disease in her final years, so we moved her from Oregon down to Texas to live with our family. We quickly learned that she preferred to stay in lighted areas and grew agitated in dark places. Perhaps it's because she had lived through many long, dark winters in Finland and then moved to the cloudy, rainy northwest where the sun seldom shone. Or perhaps she was trying to clear up the darkness and confusion her mind was whirling in. Daily she suggested that we cut down the trees in our Texas backyard because they blocked the sunlight from flooding into our kitchen! Each time we took her into a restaurant, she would ask the waitress to seat us by a window or in a lighted area. If such a table was unavailable, we would have to leave because the darkness would make her feel very uncomfortable.

We learned that reading the Bible would lighten her spirit and prayers would settle her heart. When she grew anxious, I would turn her attention to scripture, especially the Psalms, and her smile would return. Even though she struggled to speak and think clearly, her prayers remained fluid and beautiful to the end. They flowed from her heart which Alzheimer's could not affect. Both physical light and the light of God's Word buoyed her spirits and restored her peace.

She needed to escape the wilderness of her mind and come into the light of his presence. Even then, Jesus was writing her story.

The same goes for all of us.

Jesus's light gives us an escape from the pain of our past. Not our pasts as a whole— they are part of us—but Jesus is the perfect everlasting light, even in the wilderness where his light reveals what his love heals.

We make a daily choice to stay in his light or stumble around in the darkness of our own ways. *"If anyone walks in the day, he does not stumble, because he sees the light of this world,"* Jesus told his disciples. *"But if anyone walks in the night, he stumbles because the light Is not in him,"* he went on to warn. (John 11:10) His light is the dividing line we choose to cross into or move away from.

When I stay in His light, I am at peace.

When I am troubled, prayer and scripture settle my emotions and guide me through dark times. However, if you are like me, your human inclination is to deny personal issues and not acknowledge sin. To be exposed by the light of Christ is convicting and exposes my true motives. When I choose to hide, however, anxiety engulfs me. *"And people loved the darkness rather than the light because their works were evil,"* Jesus said to Nicodemus, *"For everyone who does wicked things hates the light and does not come to the light, lest his works should be exposed."* (John 3:19-20)

As the Psalmist describes in Psalm 32:3, *"when I keep silent my bones waste away through my groaning all day long."* What a profound description of an anxious heart! Hiding my brokenness compounds feelings of condemnation while confession and repentance free my soul. Choosing to stay away from God's restoring light merely deepens my brokenness.

Yet His light is always available even though I may not always see it.

What an amazing God we have who desires to restore and set us free!

He makes our paths straight.

He writes a way out of any situation.

He writes light into our stories.

CHAPTER SEVEN

Writing Vision

*"Brothers, I do not consider that I have made it my own.
But one thing I do: forgetting what lies behind and straining
forward to what lies ahead,
I press on toward the goal for the prize of the upward call of
God in Christ Jesus."*
Philippians 3:13-14

*"When one door closes, another opens, but we so often look
upon the closed door
that we do not see the one that has opened for us."*
Alexander Graham Bell

DEBI

It took until I was in my 60's for me to understand what it meant to allow God to write my story. I had given him my past as a teenager, but I seemed unwilling to let him write his vision for my future.

It started, as spiritual growth often does, with an unsettling season.

Matt and I were struggling. It's strange because we managed to keep ourselves afloat and on-track when we were teen parents, when we had a young family, when we were paying for college. But in our forties, we hit a huge wall.

Matt was unable to work for an extended period of time and anxieties about provision threatened to bury me. We could hardly afford to put food on the table, and I felt hopeless and desperate. I saw no end to our struggles, which greatly affected our marriage. God felt distant as well. I remember sitting on the bathroom floor with Ellen, crying my heart out to her.

Verbalizing my fears felt good and being prayed over lifted my spirits. Later in this book, you will read about Matt's journey and how God brought him out of this personal wilderness season, but for now, just know that I was in a dark wilderness by myself.

I couldn't see God's vision for my life.

And I couldn't see how he would bring us out of the darkness.

I will admit: When we are in the wilderness, when darkness seems to be surrounding us, it's hard to see anything, much less a vision for the future. It's easy to wander around and try to find our own way out, but that just leads to us getting even more lost in the darkness.

It was at the moment when I felt completely lost, when I saw no way out of the wilderness that I realized that the only way out was to follow Jesus's light.

To let his light guide my vision.

And show me the path out.

ELLEN

Like me, you have certainly experienced a time or times in your life when you felt lost in the dark wilderness. A time when God felt distant no matter how hard you try to connect with him. These times are full of confusion and uncertainty. These are the wilderness times which some refer to as "the dark night of the soul." The Psalmist who wrote Psalm 88 must have been in such a time when he cried, *"Oh Lord, why do you cast my soul away? Why do you hide your face from me?"* (verse 14)

I am convinced that these difficult seasons are exactly when God is picking up the pen to start writing our stories. Before he can do that, we have to let go of previous conceptions of what we want our vision to be and allow him to cast his vision for us.

One of these seasons for me was college, a very difficult, lengthy period, yet when God opened my eyes widely to him. I had come to college with an immature faith, running away to escape an abusive, controlling boyfriend. I had little understanding of faith except that Jesus died for my sins, but I lacked bible knowledge by which to combat the lies I was being taught in the psychology department. Not understanding who God was, or my identity in him, I began to whirl in guilt and shame, and in deep seated feelings of unworthiness.

I experienced an unshakable anxiety that stayed with me for weeks upon end. My greatest fear was that I had already made myself unacceptable to God while at the same time I sensed God pulling me to him. Years down the road, I can still relate to the Psalmist's words in Psalm 102: 5-8:

> *"My wounds stink and fester because of my foolishness, I am utterly bowed down and prostrated; all the days I go about mourning for my sides are filled with burning, and there is no soundness in my flesh. I am feeble and crushed. I groaned because of the tumult of my heart."* (verses 5-8)

I recently read through personal journals I had written during this season in college. Deceptive ideas jumped out on every page. So did fear. I lived in a nagging worry about rejection by God and by others. There on the pages, I read about a clear longing to be loved – words that flowed from lies I was being taught in class as well as lies the enemy of my soul whispered to me within. This led to months of despair I could not free myself from. I genuinely feared that my life was ruined. I was chained in anxiety that

ELLEN SCHUKNECHT *with* DEBI JOLMA

threatened to choke the life out of me. While I never personally considered suicide, I understand how a need to escape tormenting despair would drive individuals to end their lives as the only solution.

My own vision wasn't enough.

But God was.

I am eternally grateful that God brought friends into my life who helped me embrace his Truth for myself. I well remember the evening when I knelt by my bedside and embraced personal forgiveness in Christ, that he loved me despite my mistakes, despite my shortcomings, despite my weaknesses. I felt his presence as he drew me into the light of his love. He bound up my broken heart. He set me free from the chains of anxiety. He took the ashes of my life and transformed them into something beautiful. He saturated me with the oil of gladness and pulled me out of mourning. He brought praise to my lips. He clothed me with garments of salvation and covered me with the robe of righteousness. Whenever I read Isaiah 6, I think back to this time in my life when these verses became reality to me. (Isaiah 61)

God used this lengthy period of personal struggle to remove lies about who I thought I had become. This season took off blinders and led me to earnestly desire God's presence. I first had to experience darkness to see his light and learn to walk in a God-breathed identity. I had been living in a false sense of self and found it impossible to experience peace or communion with God in this state. Instead, I would wake up anxious, spend the day whirling in anxiety, and fall asleep exhausted from anxiety. But no one knew. I covered up my despair with a smile and friendly manner, hiding what was going on inside of me. I lived behind secret walls and tried desperately to be who others wanted me to be.

I am so grateful that his light shone into my darkness, which dissipated in his light. (John 1:5) I had to go through this wilderness season to learn how to thrive freely in Christ.

In *The Purpose Driven Life*, Rick Warren writes, *"To mature your friendship (with him), God will test it with periods of seeming separation, times when it feels as if he has abandoned or forgotten you. God feels a million miles away. St. John of the Cross referred to these days of spiritual dryness, doubt, and estrangement from God as 'the dark night of the soul.' Henri Nouwen called them 'the ministry of absence.' A.W. Tozer called them 'the ministry of the night.' Others refer to 'the winter of the heart."*

Why does God allow darkness to invade our hearts at times? Perhaps it's because we must learn that faith is more than how we feel - that we are to seek God and not merely an experience, and to trust God and not our feelings. *"His presence is too profound to be measured by mere emotions"*, writes Rick Warren. After going through my own "dark night of the soul," not once but several times I have learned that whatever I am going through does not change the character of God. Nor does it mean that his presence has left me. The journeys through these seasons have felt long and difficult, but in hindsight, I see God's hand clearly in both allowing them, showing me necessary changes to make, and in pulling me out.

He is always with us, even in the darkest of seasons. We can be confident of that. There's light at the end of the tunnel! A clear picture of this is found in words penned by Frances J. Roberts, who is known for her collections of devotionals called *Come Away My Beloved*. Her work is a source of encouragement and strength to me, especially during difficult times.

> *Behold, I am near at hand to bless you, and I will surely give*
> *to you out of the abundance of heaven. For my heart is open*
> *to your cry; yes, when you cry to Me in the night seasons, I am*
> *alert to your call and when you search after Me, the darkness*
> *will not hide My face; it will be as the stars which shine more*
> *brightly in the deep of the night. Even so it shall be. In the*
> *night of spiritual battle, there I will give you fresh revelations*
> *of Myself, and you shall see Me more clearly than you could in*

the sunlight of ease and pleasure. Man by nature chooses the day and shuns the night; but I say to you, I shall make your midnight a time of great rejoicing, and I will fill the dark hour with songs of praise. Yes, with David, you shall rise at midnight to sing. It has been written, "Joy comes in the morning," but I will make your song break out in the night. For he who lifts the shout of faith and praise in the night, to him there shall be joy in the morning.

I strongly encourage you to pick up a copy of *Come Away My Beloved* to read when your soul is feeling the most lost.

One thing I've learned: At every crossroads, we can choose to follow God's will or go our own way. We can choose to follow his light, or stay in the darkness of our own story, our own wilderness. Sometimes, our actions land us in dark valleys but at times we wind up in troubling places due to no fault of our own. But regardless, when we are in the darkness, our only hope is to seek God's light.

A few years ago, Glen and I visited some relatives in Finland. After a wonderful trip, Glen and I had turned in our rental car and planned to spend time walking around beautiful downtown Helsinki one last time before flying home.

Just as we were climbing the steps to the Helsinki cathedral, my left eye went dark. It wasn't like a gradual darkness or a pain but literally I was seeing the entire city one instant and the next all I could see was pure darkness.

Panic ensued as I strained for even a ray of light in that eye, but I saw nothing. Dreadful "*what ifs*" began to engulf my mind and heart. *Would my other eye follow suit? Would my vision ever be restored in this eye?*

Glen called a cab and we raced to the hospital where we learned that my left retina had a severe tear, and a vitrectomy was necessary to save my eye. So there I was in a foreign country, away from my family, facing a terrifying surgery and a weeks-long recovery. The doctor recommended that I catch a flight home for the surgery, one that would have prevented me from flying for weeks.

The next day, following a fretful trip back to Austin, an eye specialist performed the surgical procedure, removing the mass of blood from my eyeball and repairing the retina. A gas bubble was then placed inside the eye, which slowly shrank as my body began producing the vitreous fluid again. This shrinking gas bubble impacted my sight and equilibrium greatly for six weeks.

The strange pressure and changing vision made me feel very agitated– almost worse than the darkness. Yet in this strange and dark season, I felt God's presence in new and deeper ways. Even though I felt as if I was walking in a dark valley, he was with me, comforting me through to the other side. Finally, my vision was restored and even the doctor was surprised at the complete recovery.

My recovery was actually more than complete– not only was I physically healed, but God used that time to bring emotional and spiritual healing as well. He helped me to have a vision for what was to come, and to see his hand in it all. (And, as an added reminder as to how much God is in every detail, at the start of that trip, we had received a large cash reimbursement for taking up the offer to fly out a day later. The amount we received was the exact amount of our medical costs for the repair of this eye.)

God is writing our stories, even when we can't see where we are going.

And God is orchestrating every move.

There is no wilderness that he can't get us out of.

But how do we get into the wilderness in the first place?

Sometimes it's just the way life is. These things happen, and while it's tempting to try to think of what we could have done to make things different; the truth is that sometimes, darkness comes regardless of what we do.

At times, fear and worry can sink us into dark holes. During the first few years working at Veritas Academy, I would wake up at night, after a particularly stressful day, in a panic. My heart would beat rapidly as frightening thoughts flooded my mind. I soon realized the spiritual nature of these attacks, and began to claim out loud, *"In the name of Jesus, leave me alone,"* and the crushing anxiety would leave. Then I would lay down in peace and resume sleeping. Darkness trembles at the name of Jesus! Satan's lies cannot hold up in his light.

It's tempting to blame the bad things that happen to us on outside forces. And at times, we are deceived into darkness by the lies of the enemy. Looking back on my life, I see numerous times that Satan has lured me into darkness by his deceiving ways, and then kept me there with more lies.

Satan's aim is to create havoc both within us and in our relationships. He wants us to be defeated, weak and defenseless instead of thriving in our secure identity in Christ. He wants us to hide where our safety is merely an illusion and anxiety is growing instead. He wants us to withdraw and distance ourselves from others.

Satan fights against us with arrows of deceit that he aims at our hearts. Scripture tells us that our battle is in the heavenly realms, yet these battles take place in how we think, how we feel and how we view ourselves- and others. We can, and must, say no to his lies and *"cast off darkness and put on the armor of light."* (Romans 13:12) We are more than conquerors through Jesus whose Spirit resides within us. Jesus said,

> *"He was a murderer from the beginning, and does not stand in the truth, because there is no truth in him. When he lies, he speaks out of his own character, for he is a liar and the father of lies".* (John 8:44)

Satan spews lies about who God is, who we are, and about the world we live in. He wants us to assume that freedom is found in doing whatever feels good to ourselves. *"You do you"* is a mantra of our times just as it was back in the time of the judges when everyone did what was right in their own eyes. (Judges 21:25) Brett McCracken states in *The Wisdom Pyramid* that *"if we are all self-made projects whose destinies are wholly ours to discover and implement, life becomes a rat race of performative individuality."* What senseless anxiety this causes our youth today. God's ways run counter to the ways of the world and Proverbs 26:12 tells us that there is no more hope for a fool than for a man who is wise in his own eyes.

Satan also wants us to think we each can become whoever we want to be- without conforming to anything outside of oneself. These ideas, which are prevalent today, have been espoused through the ages by philosophers like Friedrich Nietzsche who advocated for individuals to create themselves and throw away any concept of morality that a creator would impose on them. With no God-given beginning or destiny, we have no transcendent moral standards or virtues to which we need to conform. Carl R. Truman, author of *The Rise and Triumph of the Modern Self*, writes, *"When teleology is dead and self-creation is the name of the game, then the present moment and the pleasure it can contain become the keys to eternal life."* (pg. 9) What an anxious way to live!

The point of everything I just said is simple: Satan will lead you the exact opposite direction from God's vision.

He robs us of God's light and steals away our paths out of the wilderness.

But there is no place too far or too dark for God.

Early on as a new believer, I viewed my life as if I was under the thumb of God. I believed that any wrongdoing or wrong thinking would remove me from his presence. Essentially, I convinced myself that he was going to throw me out into the wilderness if I didn't behave perfectly. At the same time, I assumed blessings would follow when I performed perfectly.

This faulty view eventually wore me down.

I was constantly striving to be perfect for others, for myself, but not necessarily for God.

I was deeply convicted by Moses's warning to the Israelites in Deuteronomy 9:5 to not say in my heart *"it is because of my righteousness that the Lord has brought me to possess this land."* Learning to absorb this truth restored life to me. But deception can die a slow death or morph into other lies.

While I understood that my salvation was by God's grace, I made up my mind to say yes to any request of me, believing that was what surrender means. And so I overdid it. Again and again I did everything I could to be all things to all people and in turn, became anxious and frustrated.

It was the same lie I had been telling myself for years, concealed in a different way. I believed that my salvation was not in Christ alone, but in my doing as well. I would go overboard in helping others and accommodating their requests, making their issues my own in some weird attempt to feel worthy of God's vision for me.

But we all know that vision was there all along.

I wasn't worthy, but he was.

I am learning to stand firmly in the truth that I am saved because of Christ plus nothing. Knowing that my salvation is a free gift of God enables me to thrive in any circumstance.

Later in adulthood, I fell prey to still another lie, a very prideful one. I was faithful in reading the Bible but with the aim of finding principles to teach to others. I wanted to know more about God, not for myself necessarily, but instead for what I could give to others. The more I began to view the Bible as a resource, the less it penetrated my own heart. I found great wisdom in the scriptures and grew in my knowledge of God but struggled personally to comprehend his love for me.

I wanted to find His vision for others but struggled to find it for myself.

While the Bible is the greatest source of wisdom we can point others to, I began to look for what God was saying directly to my own heart as well. The more I listened to how he was speaking to me, the deeper these truths began to penetrate and change me. Then, what I shared with others resonated at a deeper level, because it had become authentic and real in me.

His light is meant to cleanse our hearts from darkness, not condemn us for it. God wants to open our eyes so that we will turn from darkness to light, from the power of Satan to the life-giving love of God. (Acts 26:18) His word can illuminate every area of our lives, exposing lies, cutting through the issues so that we gain freedom, peace, and life. *"For the word of God is living and active, sharper than any two-edged sword, piercing to the division of soul and of spirit, of joints and of marrow, and discerning the thoughts and intentions of the heart."* (Hebrews 4:12)

Our loving God is a consuming fire that burns up all that is false leaving only what can abide in the light. In the light, he remakes and refines the person he created each of us to be. The old is burnt off and replaced by what is new. When we commit our way to the Lord and trust him, he brings forth our righteousness as the light to others. (Psalm 37: 6)

If you're at a place where you are wandering in the wilderness, lost, alone, afraid.

When your soul is feeling enveloped in darkness.

This is when you walk toward the Light.

Let Jesus be your guide.

Give Jesus the pen.

CHAPTER EIGHT

Rewriting History

"For godly grief produces a repentance that leads to salvation
without regret,
whereas worldly grief produces death."
2 Corinthians 7:10

"Life is divided into three terms: that which was, which is,
and which will be. Let us learn from the past to profit by the
present, and from the present, to live better in the future."
William Wordsworth

ELLEN

My marriage to Glen started out as my attempt to rewrite history.

While my own family was constantly in a state of frantic unrest, Glen's family was calm and steady. His parents seemed to live a perfect, peaceful life with family breakfast at seven each morning, bedtime at 9, and a perfectly executed routine in between.

While my own parents were distant and always too busy, his parents would plan every minute of our visits, spending time over long meals and having long conversations over iced tea.

They went to church every Sunday.

They attended their kid's basketball games and took them to the park.

They were steady and predictable and everything my family was not.

So when I fell in love with Glen, I remember vowing that I would make sure that my family, *our* family, would be more like his.

I remember signing up to run track in high school. I worked really hard all season, and qualified for the state championship meet in the 880-yard run. I was so excited to race, and I asked my parents to come and watch me run.

Their answer was as expected: "*We'll try to come but we have a lot of work to do.*"

To them, that was likely a placating response, but to me, it echoed as a glimmer of hope. I rationalized that if I could just help more with chores, then they would come. Yet come time for that track meet, neither of my parents showed up.

So when Glen and I got married, one of the first things I told him was that I would never, ever miss a single one of my kid's sporting events or school activities. I was going to be at everything. I would make sure my kids never felt the way I did back then.

I was going to rewrite the story for my family.

I did manage to go to nearly all of my kids' events. There was the occasional weekend where one kid had a little league game and another had a swim meet, but as a general rule, I was at everything. And I still hate it when I have to miss an event for one of my grandkids. These events are such sources of joy to me.

But they aren't the end all.

Because try as I may, I can't rewrite history. I cannot erase the hurt I felt back when my parents didn't show up to my track meets, and likewise, I cannot ensure that my own kids and grandkids never feel that way.

I can, however, allow God to rewrite history.

He can redeem even the toughest story.

He can. And he does.

The truth is, we all have stories. We all have a past. We all have made mistakes. We all have tried to write our own stories and found them fraught with pain.

But we all have a chance to hand over the pen to Jesus.

Like all of us, my husband Glen has a story. His story is one of a so-called "perfect" childhood. From the outside, his family looked "perfect". He grew up in a cute little 3-bedroom ranch-style house in the suburbs of San Francisco. His dad had a well-paying job at a local company that worked on the national defense, and his mom stayed home with the kids except for the limited hours she spent each week as the librarian at her boy's school. They attended church every weekend, football games every Friday night and grilled chicken on the patio on summer evenings.

This "perfect" facade was part of what attracted me to Glen. I felt like if I married him, I could create my own "perfect" family and "perfect" life.

Spoiler alert: They weren't perfect. Like all of us, Glen's story holds struggles and pain and confusion. That perfect facade was just that... a facade. And like so many of us, Glen tried to rewrite his story to erase it.

Glen shared with me early in our marriage that his mom was the epitome of a servant hearted wife and mother. She served a huge hot breakfast to him before school each morning. After school, Glen and his brother got a "hot snack" -- often homemade hamburgers and fries. In the evening, they were served a home cooked dinner and mouthwatering dessert. Afterwards, his mom would wash the dishes and clean up the kitchen by herself, not allowing her boys to help.

Her servant heartedness was good in ways– she selflessly served her sons and husband in a way that showed love and compassion.

But it was also harmful. She pampered and cared for her family to her detriment. She was often exhausted and alone, and while her family relaxed, she cleaned and cooked and served. She shared late in her life that she seemed to lose herself in serving her family.

Her sons and husbands assumed that was the normal way to treat someone, so Glen entered our marriage expecting the same thing from me. As you can certainly surmise from reading my story, this didn't work out well.

I had a tendency to want to serve and fix everything. And Glen had a tendency to expect to be served.

This caused a lot of heartache and pain for many years, pain we are still healing from.

This all came to a head as Glen's mom died of lung cancer at the age of 69. It was a shocking and devastating illness– she had never smoked a cigarette, yet her lungs had been ravaged. At the very end of her life, she no longer had the energy to take care of his father. She even lacked the energy to care for herself.

As we watched her decline, we were obviously devastated. Each of us wanted to help her, to do something, but Glen's dad's heart was very hard. He grew angry and treated her with disdain. He had grown so comfortable with the facade of perfection that when his wife was no longer able to keep up pretenses, he struggled. Rather than show her love and compassion, he would criticize her. Rather than serve her, he would disappear for hours playing golf or hanging out with friends. Rather than help her, he would humiliate her.

Glen watched this all with wide eyes. And it brought him to his knees.

It was then that Glen and I started having conversations about our own stories, and our own feeble attempts to rewrite history. We talked about how we had both entered our marriage expecting a certain story. We had both done everything we could to write our story and our marriage the way we wanted it, the way we hoped it would be.

But God had other plans.

At the very end of her life, Glen's dad seemed to realize what he was doing to his wife. He brought her two dozen red roses, symbolizing his love for her. These two dozen roses, dried and withered, remained on a table in the hallway to his house for years after her death. He never threw them away, and we found them still on that table after he died a few years later. Perhaps they reminded him that he did try to reconcile with his servant-hearted wife, whom he had let down when her health failed.

Glen remained angry at his dad for a long time.

That anger was painful, but it also brought redemption in our own marriage. Watching how his dad treated his mom at the end of her life seemed to ignite a passion in Glen to see me differently and to become more of a servant himself.

This anger pushed him to hand over the pen to Jesus. To let him write the story of our marriage.

Anger can be redemptive. Glen's anger at his father spurred him to be more Christlike and to seek reconciliation in our marriage. Ultimately that anger also spurred him to forgive his dad and to let God rewrite history.

I would be remiss if I didn't explain that anger can have the opposite effect. If not handed to God, anger can be destructive and divisive.

I've seen that as I've tried to rewrite my own history.

When angered, my own dad would explode saying regrettable things and even resort to physical aggression towards his children. Fortunately, these explosions were not regular occurrences, and his aggression was most often limited to spankings and hair pulling, but his anger still had an impact.

As a young parent of three active kids, at times, I would explode in anger as well. Each time I exploded, shame would grip my heart, and I would vow never to let anger get the best of me again. Nevertheless, the cycle continued until I fully surrendered this bent to the Lord and let him heal the broken places.

A wall of pride prevented me from admitting what bothered me, so I avoided the truth of my own vulnerability. I tried to write my own story, but I ended up writing a facade. Pride kept me from acknowledging that others and past experiences could affect me, and pride made me think I could gain self-control over my emotions on my own.

I was wrong.

Anger is a secondary emotion, a red flag emerging out of something else. Often it's fear or rejection. When Glen criticized or expressed disappointment in me, anger would flare up, but deep inside it was a fear of not being good enough. When my children were disobedient, fear about my own inadequacies as a parent caused me to explode. Glen would often grow angry when it was time to pay bills, accusing me of spending foolishly, but it was fear of provision and feeling inadequate as a provider that triggered his anger.

This kind of anger isn't from God, but instead, stems from our own human emotions.

It stems from us writing our own stories.

But we can all escape this.

We can all hand Jesus the pen and let him rewrite history.

The emotions that come will indicate what God yearns for in each of our stories – for justice, for truth, for restored relationships and for pain to be dealt with.

In God's presence, our heart's desires become rightly ordered and our emotions settle. When we are honest before God, when we allow him to settle our fears and soothe our anger, we pave the way for him to rewrite history. This gives us hope for authentic relationships with others, and for healing from past hurts.

His story frees us from a need to protect our own hearts and allows us to drop the facade.

When Jesus rewrites history, regrets no longer drive us. Nor do past mistakes define us. Every single one of us has a story that is full of regret, shame, and mistakes, but God's story is bigger and better than those regrets.

We have each been forgiven.

We can then allow God to rewrite history.

To help us to forgive others for the pain they caused.

To help us to remember the good things that happened in our past, and to learn from the bad.

To remind us that our stories are not over, and that he is writing away, even as we work to overcome our own shortcomings.

To rewrite our stories in his perfect way.

CHAPTER NINE

Writing Peace that Surpasses Understanding

"Trust in the LORD with all your heart, and do not lean on your own understanding. In all your ways acknowledge him, and he will make straight your paths".
Proverbs 3:5-6

"Come to me, all who labor and are heavy laden, and I will give you rest. Take my yoke upon you, and learn from me, for I am gentle and lowly in heart, and you will find rest for your souls. For my yoke is easy and my burden is light."
Matthew 11:28-30

 ELLEN

Back in 2002 when we still lived in Bend, Oregon, Glen and I placed earnest money down on property where we planned to build our dream house. As empty nesters, we longed for a change of scenery, and this unique lot held our interest.

Even before closing on the lot, Glen was drawing up house plans, but the deal kept being put off with one issue after another. We both grew impatient and restless – and contentious with each other, fighting over decisions even before the property belonged to us. Despite a growing uneasiness, we continued to push and prepare for this property.

Days later, as we headed out of town for a weekend trip, I began to question if perhaps God was preventing us from purchasing this lot. I asked Glen what he thought, and he felt the same way. *Could this be why we have no peace, why the deal does not close and why we are fighting over this lot more and more?* We stopped the car at a gas station to call our realtor from a phone booth- they were at every stop back then!

Unexplainable relief flooded both of our hearts when we learned that we could still stop the deal and get our earnest money back. God restored peace and we quit fighting with each other as well.

Not long after, God unexpectedly moved us to Austin. We found ourselves moving across the country instead of across town– and later settling in our real dream house, close to our kids and grandkids.

This all would have been very complicated had we purchased that lot and began construction. We had ignored God's warning signs for a long time, but thankfully, he prevented us from writing that story for ourselves. We were fortunate but sometimes bad decisions can significantly cost us.

The truth is: Every single day we all face a variety of decisions that could cost us. Could be life changing.

When we are writing our own stories, those decisions can create huge levels of anxiety. How can we know to do the right thing? How can we know if we are making the right choice?

As a young mom with unhealed hurts and a misinformed identity, I entered an unhealthy cycle of overly striving to make my husband and three kids happy. Every day, I strove to make sure everyone else had everything they needed. I wanted my family to feel peace. Comfort. Joy. And the complete absence of anxiety and pain.

I'm sure you can guess that my efforts didn't work.

Instead, I found myself feeling anxious and discouraged, in a constant cycle of overdoing it. Are you sensing a trend by this point?

I would explode at Glen, and, sometimes, even at my kids. Fear gripped my heart, but I was oblivious to the cause. One nagging fear, which now feels silly to even voice was, *"If I ever get injured or ill to the point that I can't serve my husband and kids, will I be rejected and considered worthless by them?"*

With my worth wrapped up in how well I performed as a wife and a mom, in making the right choices and the right time to do the right things for my family. My value was continually threatened because it was rooted in pleasing others, not Christ. In all this God was working on my heart to free me from false identities and the anxiety-ridden darkness they led me into.

This part of my story is full of anxiety, of stress, of overthinking. And it's starkly missing peace.

Before Glen and I were planning to build our dream house on the beautiful lot I described earlier, I landed a position as the first headmaster of a private start up school in Oregon. I considered myself equipped to handle major challenges and this certainly presented itself as one. In just a few years, the school grew into a flourishing community, but after six years of striving to please everyone – the board, the teachers, the parents, and the students - I completely broke down.

One day in my office, I melted into tears—and didn't stop crying for days. *"What is wrong with me?"* I agonized. I had morphed from a confident woman to one who felt fragile and insecure, and I could not shake free from the anxiety and ensuing shame that accompanied a deep sense of failure.

"Fire me," I begged the board. *"Let me go. I cannot lead this school."*

I could not bear to face one more issue or task, one more disgruntled person, or one more disappointment. I felt defeated and incapable of performing any task. *How could this be happening to me?* My entire life, I had been determined to face each challenge, but I would learn in this very dark season, that my weakness had blossomed out of my own self-assurance.

I thought I knew how to write this story.

I thought I knew what the right answers were.

In fact, I had grown blind to the dangers of making flesh my strength and had become like a shrub in the desert, parched, anxious and worn out. (Jeremiah 17: 5-6) My light had gone out due to another false perception.

My immediate desire at the time was to leave the world of education for good. I was done with the pressure packed world of leading a school. However, as I would later learn, God was still writing that part of my story.

You would think that this would be the time where I would realize what I had been doing wrong and hand the pen back to Jesus to write peace into my life. But that isn't what happened.

It's a good thing I did not know what the next four months would hold.

Before the school year ended, my father passed away unexpectedly.

Then we decided to just pick everything up and move to Texas.

Before we had even unpacked in Texas, Glen's dad passed away.

Everything, literally *everything,* had suddenly changed.

Our foundation had been completely rocked.

Everything that I had so carefully scripted for my story was gone.

I no longer was sure of what God wanted me to do.

And I certainly didn't feel any of the peace I was so desperately seeking.

A few months later, however, after a lot of healing and prayer and struggle, God picked back up his pen.

I certainly wasn't looking to get involved in a school again. Especially a start-up.

But God got my attention by immobilizing me with an emergency surgery. During the recovery period, my son-in-law informed me of a new school starting up in their church that sounded just like the kind of school I would be interested in. Curious, I checked it out, and with time on my hands, filled out the application for the head administrator, without serious intent to accept the position even if offered it.

Several months later, I was extended an offer to become Veritas Academy's first administrator, a role I knew deep inside, that God was calling me to.

He had placed me right back in the pressure cooker, but this time, it was his story, not mine.

My heart grew anxious with fear.

What if I hit a wall again? What if I wind up failing? Outwardly, I made no mention of these fears to anyone, and with a confident smile, I signed a two-year commitment. But even before starting, I wanted to quit. I was full of fear, and longed for the day when I would be done with the pressures of leading a school and free from the possibility of failure.

On the first day, I began to mark off the 730 days to retirement.

Somewhere near the end of the 2nd year, I quit counting. Something in me had changed even though I now managed even greater pressures in this new, rapidly growing, complicated model of education that was entirely outside my wheelhouse of experience.

As I look back, I see the wisdom in why God put me back into this role again. He did not want my life to get easier. He wanted me to learn how to handle *hard* better by being yoked with Him. He wanted to bring me peace regardless of the circumstances threatening to drown me, not to help me avoid them. He knew I needed to learn how to face major challenges in His joy and strength – and He has enhanced my life deeply as a result.

As I write this, my oldest grandson Joey is just weeks away from graduating from the very school I helped start before he was even born. The greatest privilege God has granted me is the honor of teaching my grandkids during the school days at home in this collaborative model of education.

I think of what I would have missed had I resigned after two years.

I think of the joy I would have missed had I let anxiety write my story.

Being a part of the journey of educating and discipling my grandkids has enriched my life and allowed me to thrive in immeasurable ways.

Several years ago, I felt as if God had led me to accept a job.

For the first year, I loved it. I felt very affirmed in my performance, which was supported by great reviews, and I enjoyed the fast-paced work environment and kind co-workers. But then, my boss left, and a new woman was hired.

I quickly developed a friendship with my new boss. She reached out to me for social events, invited me for coffee breaks, and made me feel very special. I thought I was her friend and not just someone she supervised. Because of this, and because of my past insecurities, I began to focus on making sure she was happy with me. I did everything to make sure she was happy with my work. So I strived to please her and do my best at my job.

Before long, Matt and my kids began to question whether our relationship was healthy. The more I hung out with her, the less assured I was in my status at work, or of my performance. I convinced them that all was good, and that it was fine.

Then little glimmers of issues began to surface. She would undermine me by taking over my leadership roles right before meetings were to occur. She would change the schedule I created and was put in charge of. She would confide in me about other employee issues and even issues in her personal life. All the while, I was thinking I was being a good friend, yet I was losing myself and growing demoralized with how she would treat me in front of other employees. My frustration and anxiety grew, as she called me her friend, yet controlled and manipulated me as my boss.

I lost my confidence and joy in this job that at one time felt so perfect.

Still, my anxiety and insecurity kept me from ever taking a stand with her. Instead, I distanced myself. Then, on a whim, I applied for another job over lunch one day. It was a job that felt like a longshot but held much interest for me. Later that week, I was interviewed by three people who were excited to have me join their team and offered me a position.

God placed me in a place where my deepest desires were met in a job that I loved and was valued by others. The "wilderness" experience in the previous job taught me to set wise boundaries regarding how others treated me. In my new job, God renewed my value, restored to me all that was taken from me and allowed me to thrive once again at work.

I learned from this experience that some forms of stress can be helpful and cause us to grow but other forms can cause us anxiety. Learning a new skill is a good stress. Worrying about your job performance is anxiety. My first job was full of anxiety, my second grew me through helpful stress.

By acknowledging what was going on in my heart, and being attentive to God's voice, I was able to fully comprehend my situation and react accordingly. The truth is, my emotions don't align with reality all the time, but God's presence settles my heart and allows me to see and act with discernment.

My daily decisions, more so than my emotions, are what shape my attitudes and mindset. When God is writing those decisions, I can make them with a peace that surpasses understanding.

God continues to reveal Himself to me in new ways. My journey has included numerous ups and downs but in all of it I can look back and see his lighted path. Cracks in my own foundation are being revealed, and broken places are being mended. While wanting to make a difference in the lives of others, I now see how an identity formed around accommodating and pleasing others had led to roots of anxiety forming in my heart. God has used many people and circumstances, especially my family, to free my heart from this. I am still a work in progress however and have become content with a lifelong journey of learning and growing – of seeking him in all circumstances and learning how to thrive in all of them.

We are called to wholeness, which requires that we give God permission to write our stories.

For me, it began with honestly examining my own heart and the desires that motivated me. My chief idol had to do with trying to make a difference in the lives of others. My identity was rooted in what others thought of me, so I allowed people to drive my decision-making all too often.

I wanted to make my own decisions, write my own story, plan my own future.

God used many individuals and circumstances to free my heart from this. God calls each of us to surrender our own idols, as well as the false identities that deceptive thinking moves us into. When we surrender to him, the result is peace, peace that passes all understanding. Our shepherd leads us to still waters where our experience moves from chaos to calmness-from chains to freedom. God provides a way out of darkness through Jesus who is the way, the truth, and the life.

My story continues to be a work in progress, but I have grown content with life being a journey of learning and growing until I breathe my last breath. *"I don't want to get to the end of my life and find that I have just lived the length of it,"* wrote author Diane Ackerman, *"I want to have lived the width of it as well."*

Debi recently reminded me that throughout her entire story, she was prone to feeling intense anxiety. Yet she has learned that Jesus is the only source of strength and must be the first place that each of us turns to for all decisions, and concerns.

He is where our hope lies.

When you start out each day in God's presence with an attitude of *"Okay, God, you've got this,"* you will have strength and peace for what the day holds.

When God is writing our story, we know. We know that our decisions, our plans, our hope is being written by him. We know because he promised to write peace that moved beyond understanding for our lives.

No matter what.

CHAPTER TEN

Writing Strength

For I will satisfy the weary soul,
and every languishing soul I will replenish."
Jeremiah 31:25

"Courage isn't having the strength to go on -
it is going on when you don't have strength."
Napoleon Bonaparte (Goodreads)

In 2020, a Florida apartment complex partially collapsed in the middle of the night, killing 98 individuals who were later found buried in the rubble. The conclusion of the investigation pointed to faulty construction and a "severe strength deficiency" that caused this monumental disaster. Sadly, the apartment complex was built on a weak foundation.

When we write our own stories, it's like that.

Our lives may look good on the outside, but when we face the storms that will come, we have a "severe strength deficiency." Jesus said, *"Everyone then who hears these words of mine and does them will be like a wise man who built his house on the rock."* (Matthew 7:24)

When Jesus writes our stories, they are written through his strength. Their foundation is unshakable. Jeremiah 17: 5-9 holds an important key:

"Thus says the LORD:
'Cursed is the man who trusts in man
and makes flesh his strength,

whose heart turns away from the LORD.
He is like a shrub in the desert,
and shall not see any good come.
He shall dwell in the parched places of the wilderness,
in an uninhabited salt land.

Blessed is the man who trusts in the LORD,
whose trust is the LORD.
He is like a tree planted by water,
that sends out its roots by the stream,
and does not fear when heat comes,
for its leaves remain green,
and is not anxious in the year of drought,
for it does not cease to bear fruit.'

The heart is deceitful above all things,
and desperately sick;
Who can understand it?"
Jeremiah 17: 5-9

When I try to write my own story, I am trusting in my own strength.

But the truth is, I am not strong enough. I eventually grow anxious and weary- like a "shrub in the desert," parched and dry. Instead of thriving, I wilt. God did not create us to live independent self-sufficient lives, yet to admit our need for God is countercultural in today's world. Pride moves us to think we have everything within ourselves to accomplish what we need to do- and that we don't need to lean on God, or on anyone for that matter. Yet, *"pride goes before destruction, and a haughty spirit before a fall."* (Proverbs 16:18)

A strong foundation for our lives develops from humbly recognizing our need for God and learning to seek his presence in every aspect and in every decision – to wait on him.

Although King Saul sought the Lord when he first began to reign, he soon turned to his own wisdom when it suited his needs. Frustrated when Samuel did not show up to Gilgal when expected, and concerned about the growing Philistine army nearby, Saul grew impatient and offered up an illegal burnt offering himself. As a result, he was removed from the throne. Being somewhat of an impatient person, I can relate to Saul because I am often tempted to take matters into my own hands. Having learned the hard way, how this can cost dearly, I am much more inclined now to wait behind the Lord and not act impulsively or strive to make things happen in my own strength or timing.

To place our trust in the Lord does not negate the need to cultivate fortitude and resilience in ourselves- and in our children. Fortitude is a strength of mind that enables a person to encounter adversity with courage. Resilience is the ability to recover quickly from difficulties – to bounce back and thrive. When these qualities become a part of our character, we can work effectively and not back away from challenges.

At times in each of our lives, we are called to run and to run hard - but inviting God into the race keeps us from growing weary. Taking short-cuts and looking for painless exits from the race merely gets in the way of growth. We persevere through the difficult stretches by acknowledging our need for God who renews and maintains our strength. Whatever situation we find ourselves in, whether in times of lack or times of plenty, we can do all things through Christ who gives us strength. (Philippians 4:12-13)

In this race called life, we thrive best within a rhythm that also includes both hard work and rest. We need daily margin in our schedules to commune with and hear God. Without margin, I grow unaware of his presence and my strength wanes. Each day, I need moments when I step off the treadmill to breathe and silence the turbulence in my mind so that I can sense his presence and hear his voice.

Each week I need Sabbath rest, a day set aside to worship God and refuel so that I can walk and not faint the rest of the week. It's something God commanded the Jews in the Bible, but it's also his way of writing strength into my story.

When I was discussing this chapter with Debi, she said the first thing she thought of is how people in our society are so prone to taking the easy road. To work hard for something feels stressful, but when we do, the reward is great. To struggle and persevere is one of the best things that can happen in our journey to thrive.

With Christ, we won't face a strength deficiency.

When our strength is exhausted, he becomes our strength.

When we are discouraged, he lifts us back up again.

Yoked with him, our burden is always bearable. Therefore, I will lift up shouts of faith and praise in the night knowing that joy comes in the morning.

Interestingly, one of the strongest people I know is my husband Glen. He is courageous in the way he leads our family, faithful in the way he works without complaint, and steady in his faith.

Yet he has often considered himself weak.

I'll let him tell you his story.

GLEN

When I consider my life, I am grateful for so much. My marriage. A fulfilling teaching and coaching career which has allowed me to work with kids and families. The home I grew up in that launched me with a legacy of faith. My great kids, their spouses, and my eleven grandchildren!

I often wonder, *"Why did God choose to bless me so richly?"*

My life is full and meaningful. From the outside, many would say I am strong, courageous, successful even. Yet my journey has been full of what I consider the opposite of strength. I have worked through a false sense of failure and regret.

I almost feel unworthy to have been blessed as I am.

As I wonder why I live with such a perspective, memories of my dad pop into my mind. He was very involved with my sports, analyzing my performances, and pointing out all my mistakes.

His constant critiques contributed to a growing risk averseness in me. It was too big of a risk to me to do my best, as I was afraid my dad would criticize it anyway. Fear of failure and fear of letting others down led me to settle into a mediocre mindset that felt safe, comfortable, and low risk. While I was a good athlete in high school, I regret not having pushed myself harder. I made the college basketball team at a small liberal arts college, but because I mostly sat the bench, I quit after in my junior year. I convinced myself that I wasn't strong enough to be a college athlete.

I chose run-of-the-mill efforts with school as well, both in high school and college. I preferred to procrastinate with studies and stay distracted during lectures. I did enough to decently get by and while I took all the prerequisite pre-med courses, my GPA barely missed the mark to be accepted into dental school. Dental school had been my dream, one that my parents approved of, but instead I was forced to choose another path.

I became a teacher, a career that did not meet my father's expectations. To him, it was a second-rate career. For years after that, he would often urge me to seek a degree in school administration instead. That was the "man's career" -- a way to be strong and lead my family.

While I knew it wasn't true, the idea that losers went into teaching was imprinted into my mind. Teaching was for people who couldn't get into dental school or law school.

Teaching was weak.

Ironically, it was also where I found deep purpose and joy.

I loved teaching and coaching.

I was a math teacher for over 40 years, and a basketball coach for over 30. I looked forward to my job every day. I loved spending time with the students, watching the light bulbs go off in their brains. I loved helping them to succeed. I still do. Some of my fondest moments are when I tutor kids or help my own grandkids with their math.

God's story for my life was to be a teacher and a coach.

Yet for some reason, for many years, I considered it my failure.

Interestingly, while Ellen grew up in a household where faith was "weak", she quickly grew strong in her faith. I grew up in a home where faith was strong– my grandfather was a minister and my parents attended church every Sunday. Yet in this place of so-called strength, passivity grew.

A strong faith must grow on a strong foundation. Mine looked good on the outside, but it was weak.

Only later in life, when I began to pursue God on my own, and for my own reasons, did the foundations of my faith grow strong. And it was only then that I began to see the story that God had written for me– one of being a teacher and a coach– as his story. The right story for my life.

I think regret for my own so-called weakness is what motivated me to push my own kids, to not let them settle for excuses. I wanted them to be strong enough to do what I couldn't.

Now I know Who that strength comes from.

And you know what? All three of my children give me deep joy because they are resilient, gritty, hard-working adults. And two of them even chose to be teachers for a season in their lives!

Now I have the privilege of watching my own grandkids grow up.

I want to see them grow strong and resilient.

I want them to succeed, to "make it", to build a strong foundation.

So I am tempted to push them. I want to push them to practice hard things and battle through the risk of failure. I want them moving towards the bright, thriving walk that God intends for them and not settle for less.

I want to help them write their stories.

But I know that's not right.

Because the best way I can help them to be strong, is to help them hand over their own stories– and lives– to the author himself.

ELLEN

I wonder how I would have responded in Peter's place if Jesus had asked me to leave the boat during a storm and walk out on water to him. Would I have kept my eyes on Jesus or focused instead on the stormy sea?

Life can be stormy. Full of challenges.

What we focus on during challenging times will make all the difference. When I set my mind on things that are above and not on what is occurring around me, I find strength and freedom in his peace. (Colossians 3:2)

For years, I regarded fear as dishonoring. After all, the Bible repeatedly says to fear not. Each time fear and anxiety threatened to creep into my heart, I would remind myself of Philippians 4:6-7: Be anxious about nothing. Pray instead. Let God's peace guard your heart.

When anxiety remained, I wondered what was wrong with me. Was I not trusting God enough? Why did peace evade me? My anxious thoughts would carry over into the quiet, dark hours of the night, when my mind jumped back and forth from the "if onlys" to the worrisome "what ifs" in my life. Nonetheless, each time I fully surrendered these anxious thoughts to the Lord, I would fall peacefully asleep.

While fear is a common human experience, we do not need to grow anxious.

Instead, hand him the pen and he will write strength into your story.

I am learning to distinguish between helpful stress, which is a part of normal life and growth, and needless anxiety.

For example, a child will experience stress when facing a hard math problem or learning a new skill. An adult feels stressed on the first day of a new job, or when meeting someone new, or before a big life change. Growth of any kind requires stretching, whether it is our brains or muscles, and stretching is uncomfortable.

Anxiety, however, is a feeling of fear, dread, and uneasiness which impedes growth and shrinks potential because it fills us with doubt and worry over something that may or may not happen.

Anxiety robs us of our strength.

In Christ, we can be set free from gripping fear and abide instead in his promises. He has not given us a spirit of fear, *but of power, love, and self-control.* (2 Timothy 1:7)

With this spirit of strength, we can each accomplish big, mighty things.

Our lives can tell a story that only he can write.

CHAPTER ELEVEN

Writing Fortitude

"Do not be conformed to this world,
but be transformed by the renewal of your mind,
that by testing you may discern what is the will of God,
what is good and acceptable and perfect".
Romans 12:2

"Finally, brothers, whatever is true, whatever is honorable,
whatever is just, whatever is pure, whatever is lovely, whatever
is commendable if there is any excellence, if there is anything
worthy of praise, think about these things."
Philippians 4:8

When I first met my friend Kim, her oldest son was eleven, her youngest was a toddler, and three other boys filled in the years between. Yes, you read that right, Kim has five sons. Kim worried incessantly about her tribe back then. Today, four have graduated from high school and her youngest is now 16.

Her inspirational story is one of moving from fear to freedom, from wanting to control everything to confidently trusting God instead. I have watched her grow from a mom who lacked joy to one who radiates fortitude. Today she leads many other women to place their full trust in God. She is an inspiration as she models a life of faith and hope as she thrives in the freedom she has found in Christ. Here are her words as she described her journey.

KIM

Fear, unfortunately, has been a family legacy passed from my grandmother to my mother to me. To combat the fear, my approach to life was "control." Subconsciously, I believed if I could control all my circumstances, I would have nothing to fear. Being from a broken home and raised by a single mother (who was an amazing mom), security was my greatest need, and trust was my most difficult challenge. So, I worked hard at school, worked hard at my job, went to college, and worked hard through a B.S and a M.S. striving and achieving to ensure my success, manage my circumstances and abate my fears.

After college, I married my long-time boyfriend and vowed we would never divorce as he was from a broken home as well. We both got jobs and worked hard, bought a home, and settled into life. It was safe, neat, and tidy, but for some reason, I felt like I was still lacking. Finally with things in order and having dated for 10 years and then married for another eight, we began our family. I was 31. The Lord must have laughed at my need for control and knew the best way to cure my fear was to give me five boys in ten years. I left my job, cut our finances in half, had to rely totally on my husband for our provision and entered wholeheartedly into being a mom and homemaker.

Although a seemingly "trusting" move, and in part it was, I also wanted to control my boys' world. And in the early years, it worked as I was able to manage what they ate, who they played with, and what they watched. But although I controlled many circumstances, I still had fears. Was I doing enough for them? Feeding them correctly? Vaccinations or no vaccinations? Disciplining them properly? I worried that the outcomes of these decisions could mess up my kids forever.

I was worried. But I pressed on.

I just kept moving forward, growing my family, walking with God, doing my thing. My oldest turned six and it was time for kindergarten. I sent him off into the big, wide world and it felt as if my safe, controlled world was gone. Now someone else was watching him all day, influencing him, making sure he was safe.

To compound problems my happy, outgoing son became increasingly anxious, experienced stomach aches and sleep issues and he hated school. My second son also struggled with school, wanting only to stay at home.

My solution? Homeschool! That, I assumed, would put me back in control. But fears still loomed. Was I providing what they needed academically? How was I going to develop them socially? Then I learned of a Christian school that provided a collaborative approach with both in-class and at home instruction.

It seemed to be the answer to my prayer.

As you can certainly guess, it both was and wasn't the answer.

Yes, in this Christian school, with teachers and administrators I trusted, my son was better. But I still had fears of our ability to do this. How would we pay for it? How can I school the boys, ages 10 to 4 with a baby? So, I rolled up my sleeves and worked harder. But still much happened that fell outside of my control, and I realized that my efforts were limited.

The weight of this realization was paralyzing, and I found myself struggling with depression. I continued to seek God, learning from more experienced women, doing my Bible studies, wrestling with choices, and doing the next thing. I would enter a place of rest but then would spiral down again when circumstances played out different from my expectations. Slowly, however, these phases of rest and well-being took over more of my life and I began to find rest even amid difficult circumstances.

I felt like I was pushing, pushing, pushing forward, but I was running out of the fortitude to keep going.

The truth was, and still is, that I am not strong enough to write this story on my own.

Fear, anxiety, control will all sneak in when we try to press forward alone.

It takes handing the story over to God to truly have the fortitude to press on.

I now have four of the five graduated and in some sort of "adulting" phase. I control very little of their worlds and have great opportunities to fear but I realized recently, I am not scared anymore. I do not have to strive and work harder assuming that it all depends on me. *"Even if I make the wrong decision regarding something important, my God is big enough to write it or bring good from it,"* my dear friend exclaimed.

The truth in her words freed me. God is bigger than my biggest mistake, so what do I have to fear? My trust is now fully in him and not me, not that I still don't have to remind myself of this at times. But mostly I'm now living life from this place of God's perfection which has eluded me for so long and brings the peace and joy which surpasses all understanding.

ELLEN

Thinking is one of the most powerful tools God has gifted us with.

My mindset shapes success or failure, opportunities, or obstacles. I become what I think about the most. When I couple thinking with emotions, they form my reality. The predominant thoughts that enter my mind affect everything, but just because I think something does not mean it's true.

It's when our mindsets are set on controlling the narrative, on writing our own story that we often lack the fortitude to press on.

My feelings and thoughts work together in how I view a situation. To change how I feel about a situation, I must change how I think about it. Neuroscientists call this technique *cognitive reappraisal*. Our enemy knows that our lives will move in the direction of our loudest thoughts, so his most effective weapon formed against us is to deceive us in our minds, where our spiritual battles take place. (Ephesians 6;12)

The evil one knows that he can break a person down with negative thoughts. Even a few words whirling around in my mind can make me feel defeated. "Thinking is a skill and not just something that happens to us," I wrote in my book *Every Parents Calling*. "We all need to gain the self-awareness that our thinking process interprets and personalizes what happens but does not necessarily reflect reality. We tend to interpret what we hear and what we think through our experience and then personalize these thoughts through our needs and unresolved hurts."

What I think about determines my attitude. When I think sad thoughts, I grow sad. When I think negatively, I grow negative. When I think fearfully, I become afraid. When I think anxiously about difficult challenges, I can quickly grow discouraged. That's why I must confront my disabling thoughts and form my frame of reference by what is true, honorable, just, pure, lovely, and commendable. (Philippians 4:8).

Rather than listen to my thoughts, or my own desire to control the narrative, I can talk to my thoughts: belief to my doubts, gratitude to grumbling, courage to my fears, His love to my wounds. When I submit all my thoughts, ideas and views to God, the Holy Spirit strips me of all that is false. Then my thinking is brought into conformity to Christ, my Shepherd, who guides me in all ways. And my mind is set free to thrive.

Sheep are naturally anxious and taking their cue from the rest of the flock. They need a shepherd to calm the flock's anxiety and lead them back to green pastures where they can be calm enough to lie down. There's nothing like the shepherd's presence to dispel their fear and panic. And Jesus calls us his sheep! "*My sheep hear my voice, and I know them, and they follow me."* (John 10:27) His Word guards our thinking and protects us from predatory thoughts, but we can easily forget our "sheepness," and go back to relying on our own thinking. When we remain in the Shepherd's presence, however, his thinking becomes ours and so does his peace.

We have the mind of Christ. (I Corinthians 2:16) Think about that! The Holy Spirit enables us to change the way we think with ideas that impact the world around us for God's glory.

> *"For who knows a person's thoughts except the spirit of that person which is in him? So also no one comprehends the thoughts of God except the spirit of God. Now we have received not the spirit of the world, but the spirit who is from God, that we might understand the things freely given us by God. And we impart this in words not taught by human wisdom but taught by the spirit, interpreting spiritual truths to those who are spiritual."* (I Corinthians 2:11-13)

Two neuroscientists who authored the book, *How God Changes our Brain,* studied the effect of religious contemplation on the brain. They discovered that daily prayer and spiritual practices strengthen a neural circuit that enhances social awareness and empathy, subdue negative emotions, and reduce stress. They also learned that our brains are constantly changing, that the disciplines we engage in every day shape our lives, in both good and destructive ways. They concluded that everyone needs to spend time each day in personal prayer and reflection no matter how busy we are. Even if it's just a few minutes.

Prayer shapes how we think, and prayer shapes us.

The prayers of others shape our lives as well. As a young girl, I often thought about Jussi and Saimi, my grandparents, who lived in Finland. As my mom read letters from them, I found security in the prayers they penned for our family. To know that across the world in Finland, they were praying for us spoke volumes to me. Their stories give strength to my entire family because we saw ourselves as part of their legacy through the generations. Jussi came to faith as a young father through a miraculous rescue. Having been beaten, tied up, and thrown into a hot sauna to die by Russian soldiers, he prayed that God would rescue him. In return, he promised to serve God the rest of his life. Later, he claimed that an angel appeared, untied him, and carried him out. Whether this angel was a real person is debated to this day.

I see God's hand through numerous prayers that have been passed down. My great-grandmother, Sophia, is known to have prayed a blessing over my grandmother and her future daughters. This blessing has been shared to women in our family line in each generation. At the time, widowed Sophia was bedridden and unable to care for herself. Jussi's young bride, Saimi, took it upon herself to care for her mother-in-law, day in and day out. Along with three sons, she would go on to have five daughters, all tenacious women, one of whom is my mother. All five daughters came to faith in Jesus and clung tenaciously to his promises.

My aunt Soili is the only one still alive today, and although she lives in Finland, she and I remain close. She is a powerful inspiration to me and her prayers, spoken in Finnish, resonate deeply with my spirit. I love that God's message is the same in every language. Soili spends significant silent time each day in the presence of God as she waits to hear the whisper of his voice. She knows that deep work takes place in stillness and that she must remain undistracted to fervently pray for others. She embodies freedom and joy which overflows onto others.

At 82 she is still thriving.

She considers prayer to be her highest priority. *"We think of prayer as a preparation for work, or a calm after having done work, whereas prayer is the essential work,"* wrote Oswald Chambers. *"It is the supreme activity of everything that is noblest in our personality.... the hidden, obscure ministry that brings forth fruit that glorifies the Father."*

Prayer is Aunt Soili's hidden ministry that produces much fruit.

Similarly to my many family members who left a legacy of faithful fortitude in prayer, the older I get, the more I crave prayer. My mind grows anxious when I lack moments of silence and solitude in my day. Before addressing issues and making decisions, or reacting to circumstances, I need to hear God's voice. Yet, we can forget to wait for and listen to the Lord in a culture that demands instant responses, instant action, and quick fixes. To seek stillness runs countercultural to the modern ideals of speed and productivity, yet stillness is how we will become fruitful in ways that serve God's Kingdom.

Stillness is key to thriving.

My own thoughts are often the source of the noise that drowns out God's still voice. Stillness is about a quiet inner quality that takes hold whether I am home alone or in a noisy gymnasium watching my granddaughter play basketball. When my mind is quiet, I experience peace despite what is going on around me. Whether you are an empty nester like me or a young mom with a brood of little ones clamoring for your attention, forming a habit of stillness is essential to maintain friendship with God.

Of course, it's far easier to have quiet times with no children around. I clearly remember the difficulty of finding time and space for quiet when my three kids were little. What I learned, nonetheless, was that I could still pause for a minute to thank God, recite a verse, listen to a worship song, or simply look out the window and breathe.

Today, I am choosing to put my iPhone down and inhale his presence regularly, which refreshes me like nothing else can. Whether it's about writing or working through a conflict, or simply preparing for the day, I need his wisdom first and foremost to fill my mind. In my quiet moments, I ask God what he wants me to know and what he wants me to do. Then I listen to his voice which transforms my thinking and guides my doing. With eyes on eternity, I seek ways to love others better knowing that love is the ultimate expression of Christ in me. With these aims in mind, I seek to be still before the Lord. Not talking but listening. Not questioning but receiving. Not grumbling but expressing gratitude.

In stillness, my mind finds the freedom and strength to thrive in whatever the day holds.

Quiet Pool
Frances J. Roberts in Come Away My Beloved

Wait upon Me.
Let your life be as a deep, quiet pool.
Let your heart rest in My hand as a bird in a nest.
Let your eyes be still. Let your hands be free.
For then I shall fill all your vision,
And then I shall take your hands into Mine
And My power shall flow forth into you.

If you would only make yourself a place apart,
Yes, removed from the pressure and turmoil,
And there I will meet you. Yet I wait for your coming,
For I long to pour out My blessings upon you,
And I long to give you My fullness.
Only be still before Me.
Never let the toils and cares of the day
Rob you of this sweet fellowship with Me.

DEBI

When my children were still at home, we initiated "windshield time," as a means to gain some stillness in our lives with them. "Windshield time" was when I was behind the wheel driving a child to practice, to the dentist, to school, or whenever.

Time just with me and a child. No radio. No distractions. We had our best talks during these uninterrupted moments when I was able to connect and gain valuable insight into what was going on in his or her life.

These conversations were invaluable, allowing my children to have the freedom to share openly and be heard. Interestingly, it was those very conversations that also helped me to press forward, to press on, to reset my mind.

By pressing into him, the author of our stories, we can each gain the fortitude it takes to keep moving forward. In his story.

CHAPTER TWELVE

Writing Love

"And the second is like this: You shall love
your neighbor as yourself."
Matthew 21: 39

"Beloved, let us love one another, for love is from God,
and whoever loves has been born of God and knows God.
Anyone who does not love does not know God, because God is love."
I John 4:7-8

ELLEN

Have you ever felt tempted to write someone else's story?

As I wrote this book, Debi and I spent hours and hours discussing the freedom that God has brought us both through our own stories. We also collected stories from friends and family members, looking for inspiration from others. It was powerful and inspiring.

Then, Debi mentioned that perhaps we should include the stories of our husbands in the book.

I agreed. Our husbands have, for obvious reasons, played a powerful role in our lives. And they also have been spiritual leaders and helpers throughout our own stories. So Debi went home to ask Matt to write his story and I went home and got out my computer... to write Glen's.

Yes, you read that write. I wrote *his story* for him.

Isn't it funny how blind we can be to our own weaknesses, to our own struggles? There I was writing a book about how God can work in any story, yet I somehow felt like I needed to control my husband's story for him. I went as far as to write it, add it to the chapters, edit it, and hone it before my daughter pointed out as she read the book that it was clearly *my* story about my husband, not *his* story.

By this point in the book, you have probably realized that one of my greatest struggles is overcoming the desire to "over" help others. It comes from a place of wanting everyone to be okay, wanting everyone to have everything they need. But it often manifests itself in me wanting to control the narrative. Of me wanting to write the story for those I love. To make sure that it's all neat and tidy and tied up with a big bow.

I have to admit that when my daughter pointed out that I was writing Glen's story, I was a bit defensive. Everything I wrote was true! The things I said he struggled with really were struggles (in my opinion at least) and the things he mentioned he was growing in really were things he needed to grow in.

Certainly I knew enough about his story to be able to write it after being married to him for nearly 50 years!

And this is where I confess that God is clearly still writing my story. He's still helping me to see my own strengths and weaknesses, in helping me to grow.

It's so easy to want to write the stories of those we love. We want to make sure they are doing the "right" things and are growing the way we want them to. I think many of us do that. Especially with our spouses and our kids. We figure that we love them most so we must know what's best for them.

We may not know, but God does.

He loves you more than you can imagine. But what's more, he loves your loved ones with a love that is stronger, more steadfast, more perfect than the love you have for them.

He writes with a powerful love that goes beyond human understanding.

Now, before I go any further, I want to make sure you know that I did go back and let Glen write his own story. The words in this book are his, and I have apologized for trying to write them on my own.

It was done out of love.

But it was misplaced.

The greatest commandment is fulfilled by the second one: to love my neighbor as myself. But who is my neighbor? Perhaps this commandment is less about who my neighbor is and more about who I am to them.

Am I willing to treat others as God calls me to? Whether they are family, the grocery store clerk, the addict on the street, or my child's teacher. Whoever God asks me to love is my neighbor. Many of us find it easy to love those we feel an affinity for but harder with others- especially those who hurt us or treat us thoughtlessly.

To love my neighbor is about the kind of love that is a choice whether we feel like it or not- agape love. This can be true with anyone. I don't always feel loving towards my spouse. At times, our children act in unlikable ways. I struggle to be kind and patient to a rude, obnoxious person. I lack compassion for the countless beggars on street corners all holding similar signs. To love the person who has wronged me feels impossibly difficult.

Regardless, if we are to grow into Christlikeness, we are called to love even our enemies. *"But I say to you, love your enemies and pray for those who persecute you."* (Matthew 5:44)

C.S. Lewis wrote in *Mere Christianity* that when we do good to another, we learn to love them a bit more – or at least dislike them a bit less.
For example, when we choose to forgive someone who has wronged us, it
changes our feelings about them. Essentially Christlike love is an act of the
will – something we all can do. Our feelings come and go but God's love
for us does not. C.S. Lewis says it like this:

> *"The worldly man treats certain people kindly because he 'likes'*
> *them; the Christian, trying to treat everyone kindly, finds himself*
> *liking more and more people as he goes on – including people he*
> *could not even have imagined himself liking at the beginning."*
> (pg. 111)

God's love is completely different from the world's love. It's primarily
an action out of which feelings will form. The foundation of this kind of
love is a commitment to the good of another person. Love is itself the fulfillment of all our works.

In fact, all of the other commandments are summed up in the word
love. (Galatians 5:14) We live in freedom when we love God with our heart,
soul, mind, and strength and love our neighbor as ourselves. Much can be
learned about love.

I only saw my Finnish grandparents a few times in my life, but I heard
many stories of how they had cared for others in both little and big ways.
After the Finnish Winter War 1939-40, Finland was forced to cede a por-
tion of their land called Karelia to the Soviet Union, causing a massive pop-
ulation transfer as thousands of refugees fled to escape Soviet occupation.

When this happened, my grandparents willingly opened their home up
to a refugee family, sharing what meager resources they had for an extended
period. Thousands of other Finnish families did the same exemplifying an
other-oriented mindset rather than a self-centered one. As a nation, they
lifted refugees up by helping them get started in new beginnings.

Like my grandparents did, we can lift others up by shouldering their burdens- doing what we can to ease the misery of another person. *"But if anyone has the world's goods and sees his brother in need, yet closes his heart against him, how does God's love abide in him? Little children, let us not love in word or talk but in deed and in truth"*. (I John 3:17-18)

Love means we do right by others out of our love for God.

We can lift others up in simple ways each day by generously offering up affirming words- ones that build another up rather than tear them down. Offering hope and kindness to others is loving. To be honest, part of the reason I tried to write Glen's story for him is that we have some unresolved conflict in our marriage. We have both struggled to overcome some issues in our past, and we have both struggled to overcome some of the pain we have caused each other.

We are obviously working on it. But we aren't there yet.

Jesus lived in a time of intense political and social conflict. To *"love your enemies"* must have sounded like an impossible command. Roman law was being imposed on the Jews who were angered by the Roman takeover of their land. Zealots advocated violence to rid Israel of Roman oppression. The wealthy Sadducees sought to keep their wealth and power through compromise with Rome. The Pharisees, who meticulously followed the Torah, did not cooperate with Rome. Nor did they like the new teachings of Jesus.

This was the intense culture in which Jesus told his followers: *Blessed are the peacemakers for they shall be called sons of God!* (Matthew 5:9)

Peacemaking is about resolving conflict which usually requires confrontation. And confrontation is uncomfortable. We worry about a loss of relationship or even revenge on the part of the other person. *What will be the result of disagreeing with my brother or boss or friend? What will they say about me to others?* Yet, engaging in conflict wisely is crucial to building loving relationships- even with our kids.

Conversely, to not engage in conflict resolution is often self-serving.

Conflict usually rises out of becoming angry and disappointed over unmet expectations. Your teen fails a test because he did not study. Your spouse refuses to acknowledge your feelings. Your friend tells others what you had shared in confidence. When disappointed and angry, we want to focus on what the other person has done wrong or should be doing to make things right. Contrastively, God calls us to focus instead on our own hearts. "*Let each of you look not only to your own interests, but also to the interests of others*" (Philippians 2:4)

How we respond in conflict reveals much about our love for others.

Some (like me!) wish to avoid conflict altogether, to pretend that a problem doesn't exist or find a way to run from it. Avoiding conflict only brings temporary relief however and often just postpones resolution. Still, many disputes are so insignificant that they should be overlooked. "*Good sense makes one slow to anger, and it is his glory to overlook an offense.*" (Proverbs 19:11) Overlooking an offense is about forgiveness – making a conscious decision to not talk about or dwell on the offense. This is particularly important in families where we spend so much time together and regularly irritate each other!

I tend towards being more of a peacekeeper than a peacemaker.

It's been a journey of trial and error to learn when to address issues and how to address them honestly. At times I have chosen to comply with another person, even though it goes against my honest judgment - just to keep the peace. At other times, the issue does not rise to the level of needing to be addressed. I ask myself if the offense has seriously hurt anyone or if left unaddressed would it impair my relationship with that person. If not, then I prefer to overlook what occurred. If the issue is too serious to overlook, peacemaking is the right path.

Peacemaking is about addressing conflict and getting past it – reconciling myself with another person. Timing is very important. Trying to resolve conflict with my husband when we are both tired makes the conflict loom larger. Arguing with a hungry and tired child is a waste of time. Plus, I need to wait until my own emotions have settled and been prayed through, so that I am able to be gentle rather than angry, to speak in a manner that builds the person up rather than tears them down. Rarely does good come out of an angry confrontation, so I remind myself to focus on restoring and not condemning.

My inclination is to immediately state my point of view, but a far more effective approach is to first listen carefully. *"If one gives an answer before he hears, it is his folly and shame".* (Proverbs 18:13) Peacemaking is not about winning the argument. Rather, it's about applying truth and grace to the circumstances with the aim of clearing up misunderstandings and improving communication.

At other times we are expected to help others towards conflict resolution. Recently, I grew troubled over an up-and-coming meeting with two individuals who were angry with each other. I was keenly aware that their individual perspectives differed significantly, and reconciliation seemed out of reach. However, the Holy Spirit prompted me to just *confess* God's promises over these two people I cared about, rather than merely *ask* God to establish peace between them and then try to make it happen.

Knowing that God's will for these two individuals, like all of us, was to be at peace with each other, I began to thank God in advance for the work he would do in each heart. I thanked him for replacing their anger with forgiveness and their frustrations with grace. Each time, I was tempted to step in, and try to resolve the conflict myself, the Holy Spirit reminded me that my role was to pray, and his role was to bring about change. To my delight, the meeting turned out to be a sweet reconciliation, with both individuals expressing grace and kindness, instead of accusations.

Ellen's thoughts on conflict resolution have given me a deeper under-standing regarding encounters with my husband over uncomfortable is-sues. I find that confrontation is rarely comfortable even with my own family members. An issue that recently surface had to do with him wanting me to be healthy and live a long life.

When Matt came to me saying "*I want to talk to you about your health,*" my defenses immediately went up. After hearing him recommend more ex-ercise and resistance training, I felt personally attacked and angry. "*You have all this time to exercise, and my schedule is so full. Don't pressure me. I am doing the best I can.*" Later that day, as I began to consider Matt's true motives, I let down my guard and we were able to listen to each other and have a con-structive conversation. I felt free from the need to defend myself and yet able to express the hurt his words caused. Matt, in return, was able to express his genuine concern for my health. When we both chose to humbly listen to each other, the discord between us was peacefully resolved. I realized that my health is a big deal to Matt, and he loves me enough to be honest.

Relationship grow stronger and more loving when each person is able to express authentic thoughts and feelings without fear of being attacked or rejected. When Matt and I both chose to extend each other the freedom to be honest, we were able to get through this uncomfortable issue with an even deeper understanding and love for each other.

Finally, love demands forgiveness- no matter how egregious the of-fense. Jesus exemplified perfect love when He gave himself up on the cross and paid the full penalty for our sins. In return, we must forgive, or we deny freedom for ourselves.

Mercy, which is gentle and willing to yield, leads to forgiveness because it's about letting others off the hook. When wronged however, I don't feel like extending mercy or forgiveness. Instead, I am tempted to hold on to the grievance and insist on my own rights. But scripture teaches us that extending mercy is more than a feeling or an attitude. It's an active choice to lay down any desire for vindication – and to forgive instead. Forgiveness is the way we grow free of anger and bitterness. Forgiveness is the strongest test of our love. Colossians 3:13 reminds us to bear with one another and to forgive as the Lord has forgiven us. In her book, *Praying God's Word*, Beth Moore stated:

> *"Remember, God's primary agenda in the life of a believer is to conform the child into the likeness of His Son, Jesus Christ. No other word sums up His character in relationship to us like the word forgiveness. We never look more like Christ than when we forgive; since that's God's goal, we're destined for plenty of opportunities."* (page 219)

Our willingness to do the hard thing is essential in our spiritual growth, but what a challenge it can be, especially with those who have deeply hurt us. What if the person isn't sorry? What if we simply can't feel right about forgiving someone who doesn't deserve our forgiveness? Yet we will not be right until we do. Withholding forgiveness until a person expresses remorse is a form of revenge that wants the offender to be hurt as well, but it robs us of freedom and peace. Being offended is not a right to hold on to. Rather it is an obligation to respond in a Christ-like manner. Beth Moore wrote the following:

> *"Forgiveness is our determined and deliberate willingness to let something go. To release it from our possession. To be willing and ready for it to no longer occupy us. God is not asking us to let "it" go haphazardly into a black hole of nonexistence. Forgiveness means letting it go to God. Letting it go from our*

power to His. Forgiveness is the ongoing act by which we agree with God over the matter, practice the mercy He's extended to us, and surrender the situation, the repercussions, and the hurtful person to Him. " (page 220-221)

Early in Glen's and my marriage, we went through a long season of unresolved conflict during which time we stopped talking and grew bitter instead. Both of us held onto unmet expectations and we justified our anger because of disappointment in each other. Finally, we sought counsel from our pastor who concluded the session by saying, "*If I had met with you prior to your engagement, I would have counseled you out of marrying each other.*" While harsh, this conversation turned out to be a turning point in our marriage. We began to realize how differently we each approached conflict and how differently we communicated. Out of this grew a conviction that we could become "*iron sharpening iron*" and not "*iron destroying iron.*" We began to embrace our vastly different strengths and personalities, which were planned by God for growth in each of us.

And we decided to forgive.

Especially with our loved ones, we grow disappointed and angry when our expectations are unmet. These expectations can be about irritating habits, about irresponsibility, or about serious issues with dishonesty and unfaithfulness. However, we can never excuse ourselves from extending forgiveness despite the offense. The Bible is clear. Unforgiveness brings on bitterness and bitterness defiles. We are to "*see to it that no one fails to obtain the grace of God; that no 'root of bitterness' springs up and causes trouble, and by it many become defiled.*" (Hebrews 12:15)

In this life, we will not fully comprehend God's love, or how to extend his love to others, but love is the lifelong journey we are called to be on. Day by day, we can do our part in little or big ways. Lifting others up, being willing to reconcile, and offer forgiveness are overarching ways we can be his light and love in a hurting world.

In the process, we are being perfected ourselves by God's perfect love which casts out our fears and sets us free. In the following chapter, you will encounter a compelling story about how Matt's decision to forgive liberated his heart and mind, allowing him to live in peace.

CHAPTER THIRTEEN

Writing Forgiveness

"Judge not, and you will not be judged; condemn not, and
you will not be condemned; forgive, and you will be forgiven."
Luke 6:37

"Darkness cannot drive out darkness; only light can do that.
Hate cannot drive out hate; only love can do that."
Martin Luther King, Jr.

DEBI

Matt and I moved from Seattle, Washington where we had lived nearly our entire lives, to the Austin, Texas area over two years ago.

Ellen and Glen had moved to Texas nearly twenty years before, and since we had never lived in the same city since we were teenagers, having them live nearby has woven our lives together in a way that we couldn't have imagined. We have always been close, but we are gaining deeper insights into each other's lives by sharing our personal stories.

It's been life changing.

This physical closeness, coupled by the time we have in retirement, led to many conversations, and ultimately, the formation of this book.

This move also brought me hope.

While I had a great life in Seattle, I often felt overwhelmed and unsettled. I longed to leave the rainy weather behind and be free from work obligations in order to start a new chapter. In some ways, I felt as if my story was almost complete.

But God still had a lot of my story to write.

When we moved, we settled into a retirement community called Sun City, Texas. In Sun City, I am part of various bible studies and canasta groups, of dance classes and concerts. I am also part of a community of wonderful people who have become close friends.

My story still has a lot left in it.

God is still writing hope for me and my future.

MATT

Back in 2002, my pastor preached a sermon from the Book of James. I vividly remember that Sunday's message: God allows and facilitates trials for good, and these trials will repeat until one passes the test.

Just days later, that message would become my reality.

The starting point of my trial began with my nephew Troy (Ellen and Glen's son) expressing concern and anguish that his aging grandfather, my dad, was not saved. I was ashamed. While my nephew had spent time sharing the gospel to my father, up until that point, the spiritual state of my own father's heart had not mattered to me.

I want to be clear: it wasn't that I didn't care about Jesus or salvation for the lost. I had been saved years before and had spent decades in church leading small groups and witnessing to various people. But I had built a wall of long-standing bitter resentment toward my father that I couldn't seem to tear down. Every time I was around him, I changed for the worse.

I was argumentative and distant; I did not honor my father. Try as I might, the root of bitterness ran so deep that just being civil to him was difficult.

I saw no hope for a relationship with him.

I saw no hope for reconciliation.

And to be honest, I saw no hope for a future.

Around this time, it became evident that something was physically wrong with me. Over the course of a couple of months, I felt my ability to stay on track and to focus deteriorate. I had always been a high performer at work, someone who my teams could count on to get things done, but suddenly, doing my work seemed to become impossible. My job responsibilities involved detailed and highly structured work, yet even the simplest of tasks, like getting a phone number right, were a challenge.

As a result, my work turned sloppy, and it became obvious to the team of people who relied on me that something had happened to me. How embarrassing! Under pressure, the condition worsened. I began to wonder if I was going nuts.

I finally gave in and sought out professional help. My primary care doctor did a complete physical and I passed with flying colors. He then referred me to do a vigorous clinical month-long psychological analysis conducted by a psychiatrist. My 'base case IQ' was baselined. Then the ability to apply this base level intelligence in a broad range of disciplines was evaluated. The third element involved independent interviews and surveys from teachers, family, and friends from childhood up. All of this was then distilled into a final report.

The results of all this testing were somewhat surprising. I was diagnosed as having ADHD, which I had long suspected, but I was also diagnosed with something unexpected: clinical depression. The psychiatrist also concluded that the reason I felt like I was "going nuts" was most likely due to my unaddressed and suppressed childhood issues with my father. Those very painful and well-hidden issues were now right there for the world to see in black and white print.

"I am the wrong man for the job," I told my boss. Then I showed him the results of the assessment and offered to resign.

He counteracted me with, *"You are the right man for the job, take time off, get mentally healthy."* This meant so much. I hadn't expected that. Uncontrollably, I blurted *"I need to reconcile with my father."*

Crying, I left the office without a job function.

My plan was to get a quick fix and be back to work with normal functioning in a week or two. I figured it couldn't be that difficult to get over some childhood issues and get back to work.

But, as you can probably guess, I wasn't writing my own story.

God was. And he had different plans.

The following days were hard. First came the start of therapy with Ed, a Christian counselor who specializes in ADHD for adults, as well as medical help from a psychiatrist. Talking through my childhood with Ed resulted in the following synopsis: I had been an emotionally scarred child. I struggled with bad grades in school. Then at 18 I married Debi who was 16 and pregnant. At this point I had no college education, no marketable job skills or experience, undiagnosed ADHD, and no faith.

Pondering how well my journey had actually turned out 30 years later, Ed asked, *"How did you do it?"* After walking through this minefield of killer odds, how was I still happily married, with a college education and a good employment record, with two grown, successful kids out of the home, and no drug or alcohol abuse by any of us. Up to this point, my response to similar questions was that our passage through this minefield was attributable to our relationship with the Lord and our involvement in a good church and the fact that we had always loved each other.

There in that counseling office, I considered a new response.

Was there more to my story?

And why was I struggling so much then, after everything had seemed to work out so perfectly?

After multiple counseling sessions, Ed offered the first substantive advice: instead of avoiding the emotional pain, in order to get healthy I must get close to it and to grieve. *"Blessed are those who grieve for they shall receive comfort"*. He encouraged me to embrace and grieve instead of covering up my deep wounds. How could I grieve? What has happened was wrong but not necessarily my fault. My life's theme had been: be tough and not sensitive.

Debi and I had committed our lives to the Lord early in our marriage and the discipline of morning time in prayer and scripture reading was long established and not abandoned. Again and again, the Holy Spirit led me to ponder the sermon I had heard back in 2002 from James. I took to heart the need to meditate and ponder the scripture, *"consider it all joy when you encounter various trials."* And through this meditation the foundation for recovery was being laid.

Then at a two-day church men's conference, our pastor dove deep into Ephesians 6 and the need to stand your ground "when the day of evil comes." He referred to this day of evil as a specific period of great testing, of personal pain and attack – a time when Satan would do everything in his power to break and to destroy a person. Satan's goal is to render the attack useless for the advancement of God's Kingdom, but we can stand firm and withstand the evil day when we take up the whole armor of God. (Ephesians 6:13)

The Monday after the conference closed, my daily devotion included "the evil day." This sparked the question, was my current circumstance the Ephesians 6 "day of evil?" I scheduled a meeting with Pastor Jerry to discuss this further. The day before we were to meet, while meditating on whether this was indeed part of my testimony, a still voice responded, "Your testimony can include the "*Love each other deeply*" only if you right now called your parents, scheduled time to see them and tell them "*I love you.*"

Immediately a powerful fear seized me. *Run. Get out of the house. Leave now. You can call them later but not now.* You see, I had never told my parents since I was a young boy that I loved them despite knowing the truth that they loved me. Their love was critical to my recovery, yes, but it seemed as if God was telling me that my love for them was also critical to my recovery.

I resisted the urge to run and called them and told them how meaningful and important their love was to me in my moment of need. At that instant, as if a veil or shroud was dropped, my mind cleared. The clinical depression was over. Literally instantly. I know that may sound crazy, but it's the opposite: As soon as I offered forgiveness and love, my crazy disappeared.

The next day in our meeting, Pastor Jerry confirmed what was clear to me. My day of evil had passed. God was victorious.

I drove to my parent's house in Oregon the next week. Every moment of the long drive to my parents was sheer agony. I felt tortured by the deliberate pace as mile after mile passed slowly. A pitched battle erupted at every overpass with the temptation to turn around and go home. I intentionally stretched the trip to reduce the amount of time available to spend with Mom and Dad.

Once I crossed the bridge into Oregon, I first drove by my childhood home, the farm where I worked, hunted, played, and grew up. Then I strolled through the old and historic graveyard at Mayger Church with anguish. Here, the headstones with names of familiar families evoked long-forgotten memories.

I pondered that there was one missing tombstone: Matt Jolma - born 1954 and died 1966. *Why am I alive?* A frequent question asked and never understood. One Spring day in 1966, a schoolmate and I had skipped school with the intention to take his skiff to an island and fish salmon on a dangerously swollen Columbia River during the spring freshet. The plan to fish quickly evolved into a plan to drink whiskey when two older boys joined us. Late in the day, and blind drunk, my equally impaired friend left me out on a raft hanging on the side of a net-raft in the Columbia so he could return the older guys to shore.

The only reason I can't fathom why I did not slip into eternity at that time can only be that God had other plans for me. It is that simple. Later, after my schoolmate returned, I fell into the river while climbing up a long fishing dock ladder, only to be saved by my drunk friend. He bravely dove in after me and pulled me out of the river by my underpants. My life was spared, and the only possible answer is that God willed me to live.

A few hours later, a call was made to my father to come pick up his drunken kid stumbling up the road. Dad was an honorable good man, highly respected in the community, well-educated and ambitious, yet humble. Nevertheless, he held one deep character flaw: When he lost his temper, he raged out of control. That day I was a recipient of his rage, physically and mentally. And I was severely physically punished, humiliated, and emotionally scarred.

Ten years before this trip to reconcile with my parents, my father had given me a gift. He acknowledged, with mom as a witness, a small handful of incidents, the abuse plus the two damaging times he had told me "*I hate you and wish you never were born.*" He asked for my forgiveness and that his treatment of me was his number one regret in life. Dad took full responsibility for our fractured relationship, but I declined this wonderful gift.

My response was a lie that all was forgiven. The pain of these events hurt too badly to forgive.

But that day, decades later, I arrived at their home and for the first time in my adult life was ready to actually forgive. For the first time I could remember, we enjoyed one another's company. I thanked them for raising me and told them I loved them. Then, I shared Jesus with my dad. This was my way to prove to my dad he was forgiven. And loved.

The following Monday, after meeting with my boss and scheduling my return back to work, I got the call: "Your father is in a coma, it looks bad come quickly."

I raced back down to Oregon. That week we spent at the hospital was hard, full of tension and long-standing family-related issues. Yet the entire week, peace and calm filled my mind.

I witnessed my father's last breaths just days after I had finally offered him true forgiveness.

At dad's funeral, as the oldest son I spoke first. Strengthened and encouraged by God's peace, I was able to calmly, with complete honesty and with no pretense, speak of my admiration for my father and his many virtues. Dad was the most honest man I have ever known. An honest attorney. I spoke of his service to our country during World War 2. And of his modesty and humility despite his brains and his financial success. With tears, I spoke of how he could laugh at himself. I shared about his deep love for my mother, for his family and, surprisingly, for me. That because of this deep love, I was enabled as his son to transcend one of life's hard trials.

Best of all, I spoke of God's very own testimony about eternal life and the source of eternal life in his son Jesus.

In the closing months of his life, dad had changed. Despite his great intellect and pedigrees, the Bible had been viewed as foolishness to him. To him, it made no logical sense. But as his life's story closed, God respoke his living words to him, which were now fresh and relevant to my father. Dad accepted Jesus as his personal Savior, and at the end of his life, he was a changed man by all accounts. What a joy to know that I will see dad again. My closing words at his funeral were the heartfelt, "*I love you dad and will miss you.*"

And I meant it.

God is a God of restoration and forgiveness, and he desires us to be at peace with one another. God calls out to us in a still small voice and it's important that we pay attention. God healed Matt from profound pain from his father, when he sought God out and did the work required of him to restore his relationship with his earthly father. Obedience was crucial for Matt to heal. Both he and his father were changed that day. I shudder to think of the ongoing pain Matt would have had to endure had he not embarked on the trip home that day.

God equips us to do his will when we submit to him. He shares our burdens and walks with us every step of the way. I am so proud of Matt following God's call at all costs. He broke the abusive cycle and is a wonderful, loving father to our two children and two grandchildren. God can mend anything.

Forgiveness is a great healer for your soul.

Jesus is the greatest example of true forgiveness, and when he writes forgiveness in your heart, it is powerful and redemptive.

I'm so grateful to have seen this unfold in my life.

CHAPTER FOURTEEN

Writing Hope

"For we are his workmanship,
created in Christ Jesus for good works, which God prepared
beforehand, that we should walk in them."
Ephesians 2:10

"Remember not the former things, nor consider the things of
old. Behold, I am doing a new thing; now it springs forth, do
you not perceive it? I will make a way in the wilderness and
rivers in the desert."
Isaiah 43: 18-19

 ELLEN

When I was a child, my family would spend two weeks each summer camping at Mt. Saint Helens. Yes, *that* Mt. St. Helens. As my parents were very busy and at home, rarely had time for us, those two weeks each summer are some of my best childhood memories. I remember days swimming in Spirit Lake at the base of the mountain, going on hikes with my dad on mountain trails. I remember serene evenings by the campfire with s'mores and hot chocolate.

These are treasured memories.

Decades later, I was visiting my parents with my two young kids. My daughter Erin was just two years old, and my son Troy was a newborn. We were sitting outside on the deck at my parent's farmhouse and the sky grew dark and tiny gray flakes began to fall out of the sky. I can still picture in my mind my daughter twirling on the grass, tossing gray "snow" into the air.

I knew something big had happened.

What I didn't realize at the time was that my childhood paradise had been destroyed. The May 18, 1980 eruption killed dozens of people, destroyed wildlife, and pulverized thousands of forested acres. The resulting hot gas cloud sterilized the land surface and swept the water right out of my beloved Spirit Lake, filling it instead and with mud and debris. An enormous ash plume rose up from the crater that would circle the entire globe.

That ash plume rained down on us that day.

I was devastated. We all were. A place that held so many beautiful memories was utterly and completely destroyed.

But here's the thing: We've all heard about the eruption of Mt. St. Helens. What many of us don't know is that now, four decades later, the area around Mt. St Helens is once again teeming with life. Out of the complete destruction, a new forest has emerged. The mineral-rich ash-infused soil has brought unprecedented plant growth, and the new forest has created habitats for animals that were once in decline.

Isn't that just like God? To take something as utterly destructive as a massive volcano and turn it into a new forest that breeds life?

Jesus does the same with our stories. Even when our stories are so painful, so destructive that they threaten to destroy everything we hold dear, he brings hope. He uses that pain and destruction to bring forth life.

Here's the thing: The old story doesn't disappear. Mt. St. Helens still exploded. Thousands of acres were destroyed. People died. The eruption of Mt. St. Helens will always be part of our history.

But out of those ashes, hope emerged.

Each of us is living in an unfinished story.

God is writing it, and as we navigate the dips and turns, the rest stops and the steep uphill climbs, we all face struggle. When we get to the end of a particularly difficult chapter, we may think "*I made it,*" but God is not done.

He is *not* done.

He is still shaping us. He's still shaping me. Glen. Debi. Matt. Kim. You.

He has a purpose for each of us. Our stories are not finished.

He is with you even in the bad times. The eruptions if you will. As frightening as eruptions are, they sprinkle mineral-rich soil on our lives. These eruptions prepare us to walk in his story.

Consider the words penned by Frances J. Roberts in her devotion, "*Head into the Wind.*" Jesus speaks directly to my heart through the following words:

> "*O My beloved do not be anxious concerning tomorrow. You shall encounter nothing of which I am not already aware. My mercy is concealed within every storm cloud. My grace flows beneath every crosscurrent. My wisdom has conceived a solution to every perplexity. I have deliberately set obstacles in your path to test your prowess. I will not always cause favorable winds to blow upon your life, for then you would be at ease and would soon grow soft and dull. It is when the wind is high and the waves are threatening that you become alert and keen, and then I can strengthen your spiritual fiber. The storm is not a thing to fear but rather to welcome. As soon as you have made the discovery that in the time of stress and strain you have the clearest revelation of Myself, you will learn to head into the wind with sheer delight.*" (page 150)

I have not always sensed God's presence in my story, even though he has always been there, writing away. He wept with me when I miscarried. He rejoiced with me when my children were born. He walked with Glen and me as we raised our three kids. He gave us the confidence to let them go when they became adults. He has been with us in the darkest hours as well as when we have felt on top of the world. He was with us in a major car accident on I-35, and his presence assured us while our son-in-law suffered through a long, disabling and potentially fatal condition. He continues to walk with us and keep our feet from stumbling as grandparents of eleven delightful grandchildren.

We are a long way into our life journey, but God is not finished with us either. Knowing this fills us with purpose–to live in the freedom of his story for our lives.

Jesus came to earth to set us free. *"So if the Son has set you free, you will be free indeed."* (John 8:36) But free from what and free for what? If we look to what the modern world proclaims as freedom, we will fail to understand the freedom Christ calls us to. His sacrifice at the cross frees us from condemnation and increasingly from the power of sin. We are free from earning our acceptance by doing. We are free from the bondage of self-focused living. Instead we are free to live by grace in a relationship with God by faith alone. We are free to trust God with what makes us anxious. We are free to live in his presence and be led by his light. We are free to love others.

Freedom is what our hearts long for.

Each of us is free when we let God write our story. *"For you were called to freedom, brothers. Only do not use your freedom as an opportunity for the flesh, but through love serve one another. For the whole law is fulfilled in one word: You shall love your neighbor as yourself."* (Galatians 5:13-14)

We are free to confidently *"draw near to the throne of grace, that we may receive mercy and find grace to help in time of need."* (Hebrews 4:16) In other words, we can cast all of our burden on God because he cares for us.

Consider King Asa who reigned during a time when everything was out of kilter in his kingdom. There was no peace. Great disturbances afflicted all the people. When his small troop faced a gigantic Ethiopian army, he cried out to the Lord, *"O Lord, there is none like you to help, between the mighty and the weak. Help us O Lord our God, for we rely on you, and in your name, we have come against this multitude...."* After Asa defeated the Ethiopians, Azariah reminded him *"that the Lord is with you while you are with Him. If you seek Him, He will be found by You..."* (2 Chronicles Chapter 14 and 15)

This holds a promise for us today.

No matter how big the "eruption" is over our life, we can call upon the Lord our God and seek Him with a whole heart. No substitute exists for daily seeking him in the Bible and in prayer. We must conscientiously make communing with God a habit we practice throughout each day. We can do this in simple ways. Stopping to express gratitude. Acknowledging our need for Him. Lifting up another in prayer. Seeking his guidance in all decisions. To remain aware of his presence is both comforting and freeing. We do not walk alone. Nor do we carry our burdens alone. He fights our battles for us.

What is God calling you to do that will need his divine intervention or it will fail? Ask with confidence and then joyfully anticipate what he will do. While I don't understand the mystery of prayer, I know that he moves by the hand of prayer. As Mark Batterson explains in *The Circle Maker*, we are to act as if it depends on us and pray as if it depends on God.....because it does!

Through prayer we move from the best we can do to the best that God will do!

The greatest thing each of us needs is true revival which ultimately is God's work for his glory. Revival may seem out of reach, but one person at a time, God is setting people free and reviving hearts for him. Seeds of revival are bursting open in both the young and old and awareness of his presence is spreading. Pray for God to pour out his Spirit on us as a nation—to heal our broken land. *"If my people, who are called by my name, humble themselves, and pray and seek my face and turn from their wicked ways, then I will hear from heaven and will forgive their sin and heal their land."* (2 Chronicles 7:14)

Regardless of where you are in your own story, let revival begin with you by making your highest aim to love God with all your heart, soul, mind, and strength. Then serve others through love. Jesus came to give us abundant life – to set us free to live on purpose, with purpose and for God's purpose. Being a follower of Christ is a glorious thing as we participate in his work in a world that is desperate for his love.

> *"And those who are wise shall shine like the brightness of the sky above, and those who turn many to righteousness, like the stars forever and ever."*
> Daniel 12:3.

ACKNOWLEDGMENTS

Family has a huge role in shaping who we are and in forming our stories. God placed us in our families for His divine purposes. I often think of my own mom who passed away at the age of 92. Together Debi and I invested a great deal of time with her in her final years as she struggled with Alzheimer's Disease. God continued to write her story even as her life was winding down, stripping away all that she had placed her security in. In the end she was left with Him. But He was enough. Her final word spoken, just before she passed was "Jesus." God used her unwavering faith and determined spirit to shape our stories until the day she died.

Special to both Debi's and my hearts is dear aunt Soili, my mom's youngest sister, who lives in Kalajoki, Finland. In her eighties, Soili continues to radiate with the joy of the Lord. Her life has not been easy, but her life has been very fruitful. I feel deeply connected with her even though we live across the globe from each other. Her story is one of steadfast faith and a life grounded in prayer through both dark and bright times. I long to go visit her again.

As we reached the final phases of writing this book, Debi and I turned to my oldest daughter, Erin MacPherson, an accomplished author and content marketer. We are so very grateful for her wisdom in helping shape our narratives in compelling ways.

So many more stories could be included in this book. Perhaps someday we will add them. I think of my paternal grandmother Kate. Her family immigrated to the states from Finland when she was a young child. While her growing up years wound up being full of tragedy, she grew into a tenacious woman who faced her many trials with "sisu." Instead of complaining, she chose to be a servant hearted person. She lived across the field from our family and faithfully devoted hours of her time each week to our large family, helping us with household chores.

I also think of Glen's grandfather, Albert Felberg, who, as a young German boy, survived a Russian gas chamber and lived on the streets until he was reunited with him family after the end of the first world war. His legacy lives on in the life of my children and grandchildren as someone, despite hardship, who dedicated his life to serving God in multiple roles, including as president of a seminary and as pastor of a large church in California.

Consider your own stories. Write them down. But remember to give Jesus the pen. We can be confident, as people who love God, that He makes all things work together for our good. (Romans 8:28)

FREEDOM IN HIS STORY
Discussion Questions

1. In which ways do you struggle to hand Jesus the pen and instead find yourself trying to write your own story by trusting in your strength and wisdom? (*Chapter One*)

2. Like Ellen, are there ways in which you over do things and wind up feeling overwhelmed – such as over helping, over accommodating, over pleasing, over working, over thinking, etc.? (*Chapter Two*)

3. A longing to be loved and accepted drove teenage Debi into the arms of Matt. In what ways does this deep human longing drive you? (*Chapter Three*)

4. What lies have you believed about yourself that you wish to grow free of? Who does God say you are? Spend time in stillness before God and ask Him what He wants you to know about yourself. (*Chapter Four*)

5. Concealing one's personal struggles creates barriers and heightens anxiety, whereas sharing one's burdens promotes connectedness and healing. What defenses have you put up in an attempt to feel safe How have these barriers impacted your relationships? *(Chapter Five and Six)*

6. Have you experienced a long wilderness season, one in which God has felt distant and you struggle to see His light? (*Chapter Seven*)

7. In which ways have you tried to rewrite your own history? (Chapter Eight)

8. We often struggle through trials but afterwards can look back and see God's plan in them. Are there ways in your life is different and better from what you envisioned beforehand? (*Chapter Nine*)

9. Do you have margin in your life to hear from God, or are your days, for the most part, too hurried to stop and listen? If so, what changes can you make to create margin into your daily schedule? (*Chapter Ten*)

10. How would you have responded in Peter's place if Jesus had asked you to leave the boat during a storm and walk out on water to him? (*Chapter Ten*)

11. In which ways, does fear influenced your relationship with your children? Your spouse? (*Chapter Eleven*)

12. Do you tend to become defensive when others challenge you? If so, how does this affect your relationships? Do you tend towards being more of a peacekeeper or a peacemaker? (*Chapter Twelve*)

13. Matt's life changed when he obeyed God's command to forgive his dad. How has the choice to forgive freed your own heart? Take time to pray fully consider if God is asking you to forgive someone today? (*Chapter Thirteen*)

14. What is God calling you to do that will need his divine intervention or it will fail? (*Chapter Fourteen*)

OTHER BOOKS BY THE AUTHOR:

Free to Parent: Escape Parenting Traps and Liberate Your Child's Spirit, by Ellen Schuknecht and Erin MacPherson and released by Family Wings in 2014

A Spiritual Heritage: Connecting Kids and Grandkids to God and Family, by Glen and Ellen Schuknecht and released by Kregel publications in 2017

Put the Disciple into Discipline: Parenting with Love and Limits, by Erin MacPherson with Ellen Schuknecht and released by Faith Words in 2017.

Every Parent's Calling: to educate and disciple your child, by Ellen Schuknecht. Released by Riverstone Group Publishing in 2022

Made in the USA
Columbia, SC
25 October 2024

44598200R00080